LINCOLN CHRISTIAN COLLEGE AND SEMINARY

P9-CFJ-795

A
MIGHTY LONG
JOURNEY

A
MIGHTY LONG
JOURNEY

REFLECTIONS ON RACIAL
RECONCILIATION

Timothy George
Robert Smith, Jr.
EDITORS

BROADMAN
&HOLMAN
PUBLISHERS

Nashville, Tennessee

© 2000 by Timothy George and Robert Smith Jr.
All rights reserved. Printed in the United States of America

0-8054-1820-2

Published by Broadman & Holman Publishers, Nashville, Tennessee

Dewey Decimal Classification: 261
Subject Heading: RACE RELATIONS
Library of Congress Card Catalog Number: 00-040410

Unless otherwise noted, Scripture quotations are from the King James Version. Quotations marked AMP are from The Amplified Bible, Old Testament © 1962, 1964 by Zondervan Publishing House, used by permission, and the New Testament © The Lockman Foundation 1954, 1958, 1987, used by permission; NASB, the New American Standard Bible, © the Lockman Foundation, 1960, 1962, 1963, 1968, 1971, 1972, 1973, 1975, 1977, used by permission; NIV, the Holy Bible, New International Version, © 1973, 1978, 1984 by International Bible Society; NKJV, New King James Version, © 1979, 1980, 1982, Thomas Nelson, Inc., Publishers; NLT, the Holy Bible, New Living Translation, © 1996, used by permission of Tyndale House Publishers, Inc., Wheaton, Illinois 60189, all rights reserved; NRSV, New Revised Standard Version of the Bible, © 1989 by the Division of Christian Education of the National Council of Churches of Christ in the United States of America, used by permission, all rights reserved; Phillips, reprinted with permission of Macmillan Publishing Co., Inc. from J. B. Phillips: The New Testament in Modern English, revised edition, © J. B. Phillips 1958, 1960, 1972; and RSV, Revised Standard Version of the Bible, © 1946, 1952, © 1971, 1973.

Library of Congress Cataloging-in-Publication Data
A mighty long journey : reflections on racial reconciliation / edited by
  Timothy George and Robert Smith, Jr.
          p. cm.
    Includes bibliographical references (p.).
    ISBN 0-8054-1820-2 (pb)
      1. Race relations—Religious aspects—Christianity—Sermons.
  2. Reconciliation—Religious aspects—Christianity—Sermons.
  3. United States—Race relations—Sermons. I. George, Timothy.
  II. Smith, Robert, 1949, May 26–

BT734.2.M54   2000
261.8'348'00973—dc21   00-040410
                                                                CIP

1 2 3 4 5 04 03 02 01 00

For

JAMES EARL MASSEY,

our beloved friend and mentor,

theologian of reconciliation in

the service of the church

on the occasion of his seventieth birthday

117903

Contents

Foreword

Gardner C. Taylor, D.D.

In the anthology *A Mighty Long Journey: Reflections on Racial Reconciliation,* Doctors Timothy George and Robert Smith, both of Samford University, have provided us with a document that scripturally confronts America's perennial, persisting, principal problem: race.

The contributors show the absurdity of the nation's attempt to be sincerely religious and stubbornly racist at one and the same time.

One will want to reflect on a great nation's preoccupation and pathology based on the color of the thin, outer, nonvascular layer of skin as the determinant of who its citizens are and what its place in history is to be. In addition, it is made clear here that one cannot be "in" with Christ and "out" with Christ's brothers and sisters. The reader will be absorbed in the path of Scripture, and of life, from inhospitality to insularity to inhumanity—and violence.

This is a book not for the smugly satisfied, but for the sincere, sensitive seeker for the spirit of the Savior.

Appropriately enough, this book is dedicated to a seminal soul in the spirituality of our time—James Earl Massey.

Introduction

TIMOTHY GEORGE AND ROBERT SMITH JR.

> It's a mighty long journey,
> But I'm on my way—
> It is a mighty long journey
> But I'm on my way . . .
>
> TRADITIONAL AFRICAN-AMERICAN PRAYER-CHANT

On a sweltering summer afternoon in July 1998, the two of us drove from Birmingham to Chattanooga, where we planned to meet the next day with pastors and church leaders in that city. The next morning we arose at 5:00 A.M. to take a walk around the city before the heat had become unbearable. As we drove down Market Street toward the Tennessee River, we passed the building that used to house Woolworth's Five-and-Dime, the scene of ugly lunch-counter confrontations between whites and African Americans during the early stirrings of the Civil Rights Movement in the 1950s.

We parked near the Tennessee Aquarium and began our walk along the riverbank. Soon we came to the historic Walnut Street Bridge, which is now a pedestrians-only pathway, and began our walk across the river. There we were, a white man and a black man, walking together across a bridge, the swift currents of the Tennessee swirling beneath our feet. In the distance, blood-stained Lookout Mountain was barely visible in the haze of the early morning light. We walked in silence, looked at warily by walkers and joggers

1

who passed us with a nod, wondering perhaps who we were and what in the world we were doing walking together across Walnut Street Bridge.

Though we said very little to one another that morning, we knew that this bridge had a history and that we were a part of it. We were connected to one another by this river, for the two of us were born just seven months and one hundred miles apart— Robert in Knoxville and Timothy in Chattanooga. One of us was the great-grandson of slaves in Washington County, Georgia. Some of their children may well have crossed this very bridge on their trek toward what they hoped would be a better life in Cincinnati and Detroit. The other one of us grew up in the squalor of Hell's Half Acre, an impoverished section of Chattanooga where poor whites and poor blacks lived side-by-side in the 1950s simply because they could not afford to live anywhere else in town. When he was just a boy, his great-uncle, Willie Nash, once told him that he had personally witnessed the lynching of an African-American man at Walnut Street Bridge. That man may have been Ed Johnson, an African American who was lynched in Chattanooga on March 19, 1906, according to the Knoxville *Journal and Tribune*.

Sons of the South at mid-century, we did not escape the prejudice and cultural entrapment of our families, friends, and neighbors. We learned to survive and to succeed, but only slowly did we begin to transcend the powerful grip of racism and its soul-destroying influence in our lives. For both of us this happened through individuals who taught us, more by example than precept, that God is no respecter of persons, that Jesus loves all the little multicolored children of the world, and that hatred is a boomerang that always returns with a vengeance on those who practice it.

These were simple folk, all of them: our grandmothers who could barely read, country preachers and part-time pastors deeply suspicious of book learning, elderly deacons and praying mothers of the church who knew injustice when they saw it. They all modeled for us the ability to hope in the midst of hurt. They taught us to keep on knocking at the door even in the midnight hour. Eventually there were others too—teachers and friends and colleagues, theologians whose books we read, historians who helped us to understand the roots of systemic racism, singers, poets, inner-city pastors, and perhaps above all, our students, whose openness to the gospel of reconciliation astounds and convicts.

Chief among those who have modeled for us a life commitment to racial reconciliation is James Earl Massey, to whom this book is dedicated. One of the premier educators and preachers of our time, Dr. Massey has encouraged us to seek the Beloved Community by seeing the world through the eyes of the Savior's love. To him we owe a debt that can never be canceled.

As theologians of the church and preachers of the gospel, we believe that the community of Jesus Christ has something to say about racial reconciliation that no one else can say. At its heart, racism is a spiritual malady. Ministers of the gospel are charged with declaring the entire counsel of God. What then does the Bible have to say about prejudice, discrimination, and favoritism based on race or class? How do we deal with the history we have inherited, the past that is still a formative factor in our attitudes and behavior? What is the place of repentance, forgiveness, and restitution? How can we move beyond pious rhetoric to constructive acts of reconciliation and partnership? What do Anglos and African Americans have to learn from one another about worship, evangelism, and social ministry? These are not questions faithful ministers of the gospel can avoid.

This book contains an equal number of sermons by Anglo and African-American ministers. The contributors were chosen because we know them to be persons of integrity, preachers whose pulpit pleadings are matched by a credible witness and life commitment to racial reconciliation. Some of the preachers represented in this volume have stood courageously against the sinister forces of discrimination at great personal and professional risk. Some have felt the sting of racial prejudice and exclusion from fellow Christians who read from the same Bible and ostensibly prayed to the same God but whose arms were closed in rebuff rather than opened in embrace. Some of our contributors have led their churches and denominations to reexamine the record of the past and to take some new steps forward in the right direction. The sermons in this book represent different styles of preaching and different social locations, but they are all confessional sermons, wrenched from the passion and personal experience of each minister.

Taken as a whole, these sermons present a mosaic of contemporary biblical preaching on the theme of racial reconciliation. Some sermons included here were originally delivered a generation ago in the stress and struggles of the Civil Rights Movement, and explanatory notes have placed these in their proper historical context. Several of the sermons deal with the same biblical texts, but in distinctive and original ways. In general, five major themes course through these sermons.

1. *God's Word calls us to confront the horrible sin of racism.* While much good can be said about the traditions of southern civility and gentility, they can also mask insidious evil. In retrospect, we are amazed that so many "good" Christians in pre-Nazi Germany seem to have been oblivious to the prevailing anti-Semitism in their society. We know that in our own country slavery was once defended on the basis of biblical injunctions. And for many decades, segregation was regarded as a divinely appointed way of life. We dare not forget this history, for it continues to shape our attitudes and actions in ways that are sometimes hidden from our own conscious awareness. The late

James M. Washington wrote that "demons thrive best in the dark intervals of human history." True healing and reconciliation will begin only when we are able to identify and exorcize the demons that hang like vampires on our own souls.

2. *The urgency of biblical faith requires prophetic proclamation on reconciliation.* Karl Barth has warned against a concept of preaching in which ministers become enamored with their own "prophetic booming." It is not the business of preachers to talk *about* the Bible but *from* it. The sermon must not become a personal diatribe or a political harangue, but it must convey, fervently and forthrightly, the prophetic burden of God's revealed will in Holy Scripture. Several of the messages in this collection are expository sermons in the strict sense, that is, a deliberate exposition and application of a particular biblical passage.

Whatever their form, however, all of these sermons move transparently from the world of the Bible into our own situation. They draw analogies from Jesus' encounter with the Samaritan woman in John 4, or Peter's vision in Acts 10, or James's warning against showing partiality in James 2 to our contemporary attitudes of exclusivism, arrogance, and lack of love. The contributors to this volume all hold to a high, evangelical doctrine of Scripture, but they believe that biblical authority requires us to name the idolatries of our own culture. Precisely as faithful expositors of Holy Scripture, we must proclaim the Word of God with the kind of discernment that will lead to repentance and renewal.

3. *The transforming gospel of Jesus Christ is essential to racial reconciliation.* The gospel of Jesus Christ has both a propositional and an incarnational dimension: "The Word became flesh" (John 1:14 NIV). For too long Christians have emphasized one aspect of the gospel to the exclusion of the other. Sometimes we have preached an exclusively "other-worldly" message, a pie-in-the sky theology concerned only with heaven,

the world beyond, and privatized religious experience, to the neglect of the real rough-and-tumble realities of the world here and now. Others have reduced the gospel to a "this-worldly" program of political and social concerns with little attention to the transcendent hope of the Christian kerygma.

Both of these approaches are pseudogospels leading to an anemic docetism on the one hand and a frenetic activism on the other. We must not divorce conversion from discipleship. In John 6, Jesus gave food to hungry people on the same occasion he presented himself to them as the Bread of Life. The sermons in this volume recognize that the gospel is addressed to living persons, soul and body, in all their broken humanity and need for wholeness. The great Methodist missionary to India, E. Stanley Jones, got it right: a soul without a body is a ghost; a body without a soul is a corpse.

"We preach not ourselves, but Christ Jesus the Lord," Paul said (2 Cor. 4:5). We do this because we believe that the brokenness of the human condition is so severe, the alienation so deep, that only the sovereign grace and transcendent power of God revealed in Jesus Christ can bring real healing and restoration.

Of course, racial reconciliation in our society cannot be limited to church activities and words from the pulpit. It must extend to our schools, courts, and prisons; it has social, political, and economic implications that require a reordering of national priorities and cultural mores. But we believe that little of lasting value on these fronts will take place until the church of Jesus Christ begins to live out the meaning of the message it proclaims: "In Christ God was reconciling the world to himself . . . entrusting the message of reconciliation to us. So we are ambassadors for Christ . . . ; we entreat you on behalf of Christ, be reconciled to God" (2 Cor. 5:19–20 NRSV).

4. *True racial reconciliation must extend to the level of personal relationships.* All of the sermons in this book in one way or

another tell the story of a personal journey from hostility, suspicion, and bitterness into forgiveness, compassion, and new understanding. As Bishop McKinney says in our first sermon, this is "not an easy road." It requires a willingness to be vulnerable, to acknowledge our own sin and guilt, to abandon old certainties and stereotypes—in other words, to be transformed by the miracle of dialogue and the forging of redemptive relationships. One of our hopes for this volume is that it will foster not only sound biblical preaching on racial reconciliation, but also new friendships across the deep racial and ethnic divides in our communities.

The two of us recognize our own personal friendship as a surprising gift from God. In coming to respect and love each other, we have been changed. Genuine, transforming relationships require honesty, a readiness to listen as well as to speak, a willingness to enter into one another's hurts as well as triumphs. In his poem, "From the Dark Tower," Countee Cullen wrote, "So in the dark we hide the heart that bleeds." But by God's grace, we can learn to bear one another's burdens and so fulfill the law of Christ.

5. *We are not there yet, but the gospel of reconciliation beckons us forward.* The title for this book comes from an African-American prayer-chant, an affirmation of faith and hope sometimes moaned by the congregation amid shouts of "Amen," "Yes, Lord," or "Help us, Lord":

It's a mighty long journey
But I'm own my way—
It is a mighty long journey
But I'm own my way . . .

Most of the contributors to this volume grew up in the era of legally mandated segregation when overt public racism was socially acceptable. Some of us were even accomplices in this regime, while others endured the shame of exclusion. Looking back on this era, we acknowledge with gratitude the courage of those who protested, suffered, and even died to advance the cause of human and civil rights. Even though the church as an institution has been painfully retarded in its own progress, we give thanks to God for signs of a new awareness and, we pray, lasting commitment to the Christian principles we believe and teach.

We rejoice in the blessings we have seen and received, but we also know that we are not there yet. It is *still* a mighty long journey, but like Christian in John Bunyan's *The Pilgrim's Progress*, we are called to move forward in faith, stumbling at times, weary, often discouraged and frustrated with others and ourselves, but nonetheless drawn ineluctably toward that Celestial City, the Kingdom of Racial Reconciliation, that Beloved Community where at last we shall know one another even as we ourselves are known, where we shall rest from all our burdens and be finally free at last.

One hundred years ago, in 1900, James Weldon Johnson wrote the following prayer to celebrate the birthday of Abraham Lincoln. We offer it here as our own prayer and the prayer of all others who have joined us in this mighty long journey:

> God of our weary years,
> God of our silent tears,
> Thou who hast brought us thus far on the way,
> Thou who hast by Thy might
> Led us into the light,
> Keep us forever in the path, we pray;
> Lest our feet stray from the places, our God,
>   where we met Thee,
> Lest our hearts, drunk with the wine of the
>   world, we forget Thee . . .
> Shadowed beneath Thy hand, may we forever stand
> True to our God, true to our Native Land.

Chapter 1

Not an Easy Road

GEORGE D. MCKINNEY JR.
2 Corinthians 5:19

Racial reconciliation is very much in the hearts and minds of people of goodwill around the country and around the world. The great evangelist, Billy Graham, said recently that he felt the greatest hindrance to effective evangelization around the world is racism that still exists in the Body of Christ. I don't think it was an overstatement. I think it is one of the greatest hindrances.

I'm disturbed as a believer in Jesus Christ and as a pastor by recent information that Islam, the Muslim religion in this country, is now the second largest religion and has overtaken Judaism. Much of the proselytizing that is taking place in Islam is in the black community and

GEORGE D. MCKINNEY JR. is the founding pastor of St. Stephen's Church of God in Christ in San Diego, California, and also presides as bishop over the Second Ecclesiastical Southern Jurisdiction of his denomination. A native of Jonesboro, Arkansas, he holds degrees from Arkansas State University (B.A.), Oberlin College School of Theology (M.A.), and California Graduate School of Theology (Ph.D.). Bishop McKinney is past president of the National Black Evangelical Association and has served the wider body of Christ in numerous ways.

He is a trustee of the Interdenominational Theological Center in Atlanta and serves on the boards of InterVarsity Christian Fellowship, Religious Alliance Against Pornography, Black Family Institute, C. H. Mason Theological Seminary, Southern California College, and American Urban University. He is also the senior editor of African American Devotional Bible (Zondervan). A leader of great vision and compassion, Bishop McKinney has been at the center of recent breakthroughs and initiatives for racial reconciliation, some of which he describes in this stirring message, "Not an Easy Road."

in the jails and prisons where there is an ongoing disaffection between many blacks and people of color about racism in the society and in the church. But there is a ray of hope. I've had the privilege of being involved in a number of meetings and conferences where twenty-five years ago the issue of racism would not have been discussed at all. But now it is not only discussed; there has been an ongoing open declaration that *racism is sin.*

Recently at St. Stephen's Church, I noticed there was a brother of a lighter hue sitting in the back of the church. He came to the fellowship meeting after the worship and said, "I need to make a statement." He was forty-nine years of age. He was a successful businessman who had three grown sons and one daughter. I was amazed at what he had to say. He said, "I want to tell you that today is the first day of my life that I have not had hatred and prejudice toward black folk. My father taught me to hate Blacks. His father taught him and I taught my three sons to hate Blacks. But today, I don't have any of that hatred anymore. It's all gone. So, I've come to repent and confess and ask for forgiveness. Now I have to face my sons and daughter whom I've taught to hate black people and tell them that I was wrong."

One man's confession and repentance released a flood of forgiveness in our congregation. There was great rejoicing as we experienced the liberating power of the Holy Spirit.

I'm thankful that the church is saying, without any trepidation, without any apologies, the truth that "racism is sin." Evangelicals and the church everywhere need to deal with sin, not on the basis of sociological or anthropological insights or cultural dictates, but the church must deal with sin based on Scripture. Isn't it interesting that if there's adultery in the congregation, we deal with it on the basis of Scripture? If somebody is stealing the offering, we deal with it based on the law and the Scriptures. If there's any other sin identified among the body of believers, we deal with it based on the Scriptures. For too long the church accepted racism and justified its existence in the church and society based on cultural norms. Just as the Scripture exposes and condemns murder, adultery, and other sins, so the Scripture also exposes and condemns the sin of racism.

What is happening all around this country in the faith communities is the realization of the truth that *racism is sin*. We don't need to have any timidity about that statement. Racism declares that access to God, favorable status with God, is gained on the basis of race, whereas the gospel declares that favorable status with God is always based on *grace*. "For the grace of God that bringeth salvation hath appeared to all men"—black men, white men, up folk and down folk—"teaching us that, denying ungodliness and worldly lust, we should live soberly, righteously, and godly, in this present world" (Titus 2:11).

I have a working definition for racism. Racism is prejudice plus power. It is the institutionalized expression of a controlling group's prejudices. *Racism is sin* and it is sin on several counts. It is a clear violation of God's law of love. It has enslaved, impoverished, and oppressed people in the United States and around the world. Racism is idolatry because it teaches that salvation is by *race* rather than *grace*. It is sin. It is an act of rebellion against God's revealed truth that all human life is created in God's image. Humanity fully expresses God's image in a wealth of diversity.

Racism is sin because it teaches that man's dignity and worth are determined by skin color and not by man's relatedness to God. God's Word declares that man's worth and dignity are derived from his being a child of God by creation. "What is man, that thou art mindful of him? and the son of man, that thou visitest him?" (Ps. 8:4). God has made man in his own image and likeness. Further, *racism is sin* because it teaches the lie that grace is selective and racially inclusive of the majority group. The Bible declares that God is no respecter of persons. Whoever loves God, and fears him, is acceptable with God.

Racism is sin because it places culture and custom above Scripture. For too long the church has failed to use Scripture in dealing with racism. The racists stand on the quicksand of vacillating customs and ever-changing laws and society's norms. But we must always stand on Scripture. It is not God's will that any should perish. All have equal access to God through grace in Jesus Christ. It is strange how the church allowed itself to drift and to reflect the prevailing notions of the culture rather than the clear teachings of Scripture regarding God's love for all people. In the life of Christ, it is quite clear, not only during his personal ministry, but in his parabolic teachings. For example, his story regarding the Samaritan was about someone who was different and yet whose behavior and faith placed him within God's favor and grace.

Racism is sin because it distorts the gospel. *Racism is sin* because it teaches that a person can be excluded from acceptance into the family of faith based on skin, when the gospel clearly teaches that the only basis of exclusion from the kingdom, from the family of faith, is *sin, not skin.*

Racism is sin because it accuses God of making some folks inferior—turning out some shoddy products. It states that God made some folks intelligent, and others he made not so intelligent, on the basis of racial categories. We accuse God when we buy into and believe that lie of racism, that God has somehow made some folks inferior—some are to be hewers of wood and drawers of water.

I will never forget when I was a young man in Arkansas. The legislature used to say when they passed the allotments or the legislation for education, "We'll keep the allocations very small for the blacks because whenever you educate a black man, you ruin a good cotton picker." That was the attitude. We lived under that until recently because racism teaches that God has been prejudicial in his act of creation. We know that it is sin because it tells lies on God. The Bible says that God, from one blood, created all nations to dwell on the face of the earth. *Racism is sin* because it gives the message that a person can be excluded from the fellowship of faith and from the abundant blessings of God on the basis of cultural determination rather than Scripture.

All that we have and all that we have received, we have received from God. Therefore, racism must be rejected because it denies the fact that God is the owner of everything. Racism and injustice are twins, and whenever there is denial of the biblical concept of justice, there is a denial of the sovereignty of God and his ownership of the world. My friend, John Perkins, always says, "Justice is the question of who owns what." The wealth of this world and the privileges do not really belong to those who have it. It is not the property of the *needy* or the *greedy*, but "the earth is the LORD's, and the fulness thereof; the world, and they that dwell therein" (Ps. 24:1). So, if it is the question of who owns what—if God owns everything—then it is rather presumptuous for any group of those who have access to another, to God's property, to appropriate it and to hold it and to covetously and selfishly attempt to deny access to that which belongs to God, which he has provided for all his people.

There is reason for encouragement for the believer about what is happening in the whole arena of racial reconciliation. The Promise Keepers movement, with which I have served for three years as one of their speakers, devoted a full year (1996) to programs promoting racial reconciliation and breaking down the walls. There were more than a million men meeting in twenty-three stadiums around the country.

I can never forget the meeting at the Silverdome in Pontiac, Michigan—seventy thousand men. There were fifty thousand in San Diego, California. There were sixty thousand in Boulder,

Colorado. The focus was "Bring Down the Walls," and it was an approach that recognized that unless God does it—except God moves upon the hearts of the people—the walls will remain, separating Christian from Christian, and brothers and sisters from each other. The emphasis for Promise Keepers seems to come mainly from Coach McCartney, whose heart God has touched. There is a commitment within him to use every ounce of his influence to promote justice, righteousness, and reconciliation in the body of Christ.

In 1995 the Southern Baptist Convention for the first time in its history openly declared that there had been sin committed against God and God's people. They stated that they rejected the racist and segregationist policies of the past and began aggressively to seek ways of repentance and avenues for reconciliation. This is especially significant in light of the fact that Southern Baptists had historically supported racism and racial discrimination.

Another significant step in the journey toward reconciliation in the church in the United States was the miracle of Memphis in October of 1994, when the historically Pentecostal and charismatic church leaders came together in Memphis, Tennessee. These were churches born out of the Azusa Revival of 1906 that was led by the Holy Ghost through a black preacher named William Seymour. Out of that tremendous revival, the Church of God in Christ, the Assemblies of God, the Church of Christ Holiness, the Four Square Church, and a myriad of other Pentecostal and charismatic churches came into being.

But because of segregation and racism in the society, those who were united in heart and spirit in the 1906 Azusa Revival were separated. It was in 1914 that the ministers who were Caucasian and credentialed in the Church of God in Christ met in Hot Springs, Arkansas, and formed the Assemblies of God because the laws in Mississippi, Arkansas, Alabama, and Georgia said that the black and white people could not worship in the same building. So, the Church of God in Christ and the Assemblies of God has a common beginning, but the leaders responded to the pressure of the culture and the temperament of the times.

But in 1994, the bishops, the leaders of the Church of God in Christ, the Assemblies of God, the Four Square Church, and about six other Pentecostal groups met in Memphis, openly repented, washed one another's feet, and pledged to reorganize their association so there would no longer be a black Pentecostal association and a white Pentecostal association, but rather there would be one association. They elected my friend and colleague, Bishop Ithiel Clemmons from New York, as the president of the new organization. This is a meaningful movement toward reconciliation.

Then I had the privilege also of being in Chicago in January of 1996 when the leadership of the National Association of Evangelicals and the leadership of the National Black Evangelical Association met. These are two evangelical associations existing side by side, separate, and not having much communication. The separation took place during the early 1960s because the black members of the NAE felt they were only useful to sing or to participate on the periphery of the agency. So during that time of the movement toward justice, the Civil Rights Movement, the black members of the NAE separated and formed the NBEA. Since 1962, each Christian evangelical group had been meeting, praising God, proclaiming their testimony, but hardly communicating at all. I believe it was the move of the Holy Spirit that indicated, "This is unacceptable."

So, while I was serving as the president of the NBEA during the mid-1980s along with the executive director, Aaron Hamlin, we were able to negotiate a series of meetings. I'll never forget the first meeting we had in Phoenix, Arizona. When we began to talk about the hurt and the scandal of being separated and the fact that the issue of injustice and racism was not being addressed by the major Evangelical groups, there was a look of puzzlement and a question on the faces of those who were there asking, "What are you talking about? We've been nice. There's no problem here." They could not, at that point, sense the depth of the problem.

Since the mid-1980s to the meeting in 1996, the profound changes, the sense of repentance, and the desire for reconciliation have been amazing. In that meeting in January of 1996, there was weeping and there was brokenness. There were people from the major Evangelical seminaries across the country. The leaders of the association were there. The leaders from the Black and Hispanic communities came. Not only was there weeping and embracing, but there was repentance and a pledge made to move forward and to do some things differently to make a witness to the world that the body of Christ is *one body.*

The Southern Baptists, the miracle in Memphis, the Promise Keepers, and the NAE and the NBEA movements toward reconciliation are significant developments. It is a statement that the Holy Spirit is at work among us to bring down the walls and to bring to us a clearer understanding that the gospel of grace really is a gospel of reconciliation.

Let's spend a moment talking about why it is important that we place racial reconciliation high on our agenda. Paul states in 2 Corinthians 5:19: "God was in Christ, reconciling the world unto himself . . . and hath committed unto us the word of reconciliation." The whole drama of redemption is about reconciliation. Grace is God's *reconciliation at Christ's expense*—God's redemption at Christ's expense. All have sinned and rebelled against God. We've all missed the mark, but thanks be to God that he has provided a remedy for sin, the notorious separator that separates man from himself, from others and from God.

John 3:16 states: "For God so loved the world, that he gave his only begotten Son, that whosoever believeth in him should not perish, but have everlasting life."

Both this passage and the passage from 2 Corinthians declare that the work of grace is the work of reconciliation, of redemption. The New Testament message is that the eternal God entered history in Jesus Christ, who reconciled the world unto himself. He has committed unto us, the believers, this word, this ministry of reconciliation.

Racial reconciliation is a vital part of this unfolding drama of redemption. While there have always been groups of Christians who have openly renounced racism as sin, it is only recently that major Christian bodies in America have opened up and declared that racism is sin and have repented of this sin. For too long, the Christian church in America did not deal with racism as sin. Rather, it was treated as a sociopolitical phenomenon with deep roots in culture and history. It was not to be tampered with from the religious perspective. The church did not own the problem. It was a problem seen as society's problem to be addressed with social and economic solutions.

Four hundred years of history in the United States have clearly demonstrated that the social, economic, and political solutions are not effective in dealing with what is essentially a spiritual problem. The universal spiritual problem may be described as alienation and estrangement from God. This estrangement from God always results in selfishness, inner conflict, and social discord.

Through Jesus Christ, we who were estranged and separated from God have received forgiveness and acceptance and have become a part of the family of faith. Ephesians 2:11–22 states:

> Wherefore remember, that ye being in time past
> Gentiles in the flesh, who are called Uncircumcision
> by that which is called the Circumcision in the flesh
> made by hands; that at that time ye were without

Christ, being aliens from the commonwealth of Israel, and strangers from the covenants of promise, having no hope, and without God in the world: But now in Christ Jesus ye who sometimes were far off are made nigh by the blood of Christ. For he is our peace, who hath made both one, and hath broken down the middle wall of partition between us; having abolished in his flesh the enmity, even the law of commandments contained in ordinances; for to make in himself of twain one new man, so making peace; and that he might reconcile both unto God in one body by the cross, having slain the enmity thereby: And came and preached peace to you which were afar off, and to them that were nigh. For through him we both have access by one Spirit unto the Father. Now therefore ye are no more strangers and foreigners, but fellowcitizens with the saints, and of the household of God; and are built upon the foundation of the apostles and prophets, Jesus Christ himself being the chief corner stone; in whom all the building fitly framed together groweth unto an holy temple in the Lord: In whom ye also are builded together for an habitation of God through the Spirit.

Let's look again at the word from 2 Corinthians: "God was in Christ, reconciling the world unto himself . . . and hath committed unto us the word of reconciliation." This ministry, this word of reconciliation is so well translated by the believers who practice love and forgiveness. It is translated into acts of compassion and loving service. It is love that has working clothes on that moves into the arena where there is suffering. It is love that's fearless, bold to address the ugly problems and to deal with human failure and dare to believe that grace is greater than all of our sins. It is ministry translated into partnership with the poor, addressing their concerns; partnership with the defenseless and the marginalized. It is ministry that translates into service to those who have no advocates—to the voiceless, the homeless, the youth who are disaffected and disconnected, prisoners, the mentally ill, the children, the older Americans.

This word of reconciliation must, in every age, be translated into service and acts of reconciliation. We must be willing to touch somebody's life. We must continue to reject the stereotypes and the myths perpetuated by racist language. For racial reconciliation to move forward at the end of this century, we must continue to develop new Christian education materials that will reflect a correction of the view of history that has so often left out the contributions of African Americans, Native Americans, Hispanics, and other minorities and their involvement in the brotherhood of man.

Racial reconciliation must include our working together for a full integration of schools, colleges, and seminaries. We are deeply concerned that in many Christian schools around the country, the percentage of black and other minority students still remains between 3 and 6 percent. We must equip believers to confront institutional and systemic racism, so that those who have responded to God's call to reconciliation will be encouraged and emboldened to do what's right in the face of cultural and historical realities.

At the same time, I must caution those who would travel the road toward reconciliation that it is not an easy road. The years of estrangement, ignorance, injustice, and the pain and the suffering have resulted in bitterness, rage, hatred, and distrust. Some of these elements are to be found even among believers. So it is very important for us to understand that there must always be patience and compassion without compromising our position: "God was in Christ, reconciling the world unto himself, not imputing their trespasses unto them; and hath committed unto us the word of reconciliation" (2 Cor. 5:19).

Therefore, it is important for us to understand the urgency of always being available to take a stand for racial reconciliation, justice, and righteousness. God is requiring nothing less than that. We must understand that in this search for racial reconciliation, we simply cannot expect those in academia or in the business world or in government to right the wrong. Racial separation and injustice are works of darkness—*sin.*

I think we would all agree that God has called us, the believers, the church, the *ecclesia,* the called out ones, to be light in this present darkness. Racial reconciliation is high on God's agenda, and it must be high on the church's agenda. He has given to us this word and this ministry of racial reconciliation. He did not give this responsibility to the government or to the financial institutions or the educational institutions, although they must be influenced by the church. But it is the church's responsibility to be light and salt. Reconciliation is God's work in his world.

Chapter 2

Moving toward the Kingdom of Racial Reconciliation

RICHARD D. LAND

2 Corinthians 5:17

It is particularly appropriate to be here in Atlanta tonight. Historically, Baptists in their southern expression have been at their worst and at their best on race in this state. It was in Augusta, Georgia, that Baptists from across the South gathered in 1845 to form the Southern Baptist Convention, separating from our northern brethren largely over the issue of slavery that was to later rend the nation. In 1995, on the 150th anniversary of our founding as a convention, Southern Baptists once again gathered in Georgia, this time to ask for the forgiveness of our African-American brothers and sisters and to apologize to

RICHARD D. LAND is president of the Ethics and Religious Liberty Commission of the Southern Baptist Convention. A native of Houston, Texas, he holds degrees from Princeton University (B.A.), New Orleans Baptist Theological Seminary (Th.M.), and Oxford University (D. Phil.). For eight years Dr. Land served as vice president for academic affairs at The Criswell College in Dallas. A prolific writer, Dr. Land has edited and contributed to numerous books on religion and public life, including The Earth Is the Lord's, Life at Risk, Citizen Christians, and Christians in the Public Square. His popular radio call-in talk show "For Faith and Family," is heard on more than five hundred stations in North America.

Dr. Land has been a prophetic voice among Southern Baptists on behalf of racial reconciliation. This sermon, "Moving toward the Kingdom of Racial Reconciliation," was preached on January 9, 1999, in Atlanta, Georgia, during the International Summit Against Racism sponsored by the Baptist World Alliance, a historic conference cochaired by former President Jimmy Carter and Coretta Scott King.

them for our past advocacy of, or acquiescence to, slavery, segregation, and racial prejudice.

I must also say to you, as I stand here tonight, that I am disappointed, sometimes even depressed, that in the year of our Lord, 1999, we have not come far enough as Americans in our quest for a racially reconciled society. I was a junior in high school in 1964 when the 1964 Civil Rights Act was passed, and I don't think former President Carter ever spoke truer words than when he said he was grateful to God for the 1964 and 1965 Civil Rights Acts because they liberated us (and when he said "us" he meant white southerners) from a situation in which we had manifestly shown we were unwilling, or unable, to extricate ourselves. The Civil Rights Revolution allowed us to rejoin our country as fully participating citizens and to be liberated from the segregation that victimized us all.

As a seminary student from 1969 to 1972, I believe that I could be forgiven for having been optimistic about racial reconciliation. As I entered seminary in August 1969, I could look back at the revolutionary progress achieved between 1954's U. S. Supreme Court *Brown v. Board of Education* decision and the civil rights acts of the mid- and late-1960s and confidently conclude that, having made that much progress in a decade and a half, we would be much farther down the road toward true racial reconciliation than we have come in the last thirty years.

My Scripture text is found in the second letter of Paul to the Corinthian church. Second Corinthians 5, verses 17–20.

> Therefore if any man be in Christ, he is a new creature: old things are passed away; behold, all things are become new. And all things are of God, who hath reconciled us to himself by Jesus Christ, and hath given to us the ministry of reconciliation; to wit, that God was in Christ, reconciling the world unto himself, not imputing their trespasses unto

them; and hath committed unto us the word of reconciliation. Now then we are ambassadors for
Christ, as though God did beseech you by us: we
pray you in Christ's stead, be ye reconciled to God.

As men and women who have come to a saving knowledge
of Jesus Christ, we have experienced that reconciliation. In verse
18, the word *reconciled* is in the aorist tense, which means that
there was an action at a point in time and that has taken place.
It took place at Calvary. It was confirmed on the first Easter
morning when the Resurrection took place. As a consequence,
we are reconciled. In verse 19, the participle denotes "reconciling," past action with continuing consequences. In other words,
in our past, in our present, and in our future, we have been reconciled in Christ Jesus to God Almighty as we are "twice-born"
men and women.

The fact of that vertical reconciliation—which is symbol-
ized by the universal symbol of our common faith, the cross of
our Lord and Savior, Jesus Christ—gives us the hope of the horizontal reconciliation with brothers and sisters around the
world, whatever their ethnic background or derivation, whatever
their skin hue, whatever their sex or their national origin. But we
must understand that the true reconciliation we seek can only
come when it is rooted in, and witnessed to, by that vertical reconciliation that we have in Christ.

We must understand the nature of the enemy we confront.
It is an enemy within as well as without. Racial bigotry is woven
into the very warp and woof of our society. I cannot speak with
an expert's or a native's authority about other cultures, but I can
speak about this culture. American society has racism in the
warp and woof of its very nature as sin is an integral part of
human nature. After the Fall, the Bible tells us "the heart is de-
ceitful above all things, and desperately wicked: who can know

it?" (Jer. 17:9). That verse is bad enough in English. It is worse in the original Hebrew because there the heart and its adjectives are inextricably connected, and it literally means that the heart of man is incurable because that is its nature. It produces what it is. It knows nothing else.

In this secularly dominated age in which we increasingly live, we who are born-again believers, we who have experienced that vertical reconciliation in Christ have a unique responsibility to remind our society that racism, as well as many other problems, will not be fully solved without the spiritual dimension.

The last half century of our world has been an evil and terrible time in terms of what people have done to one other. At the end of the nineteenth and the early part of the twentieth century, there had been remarkable progress that resulted from the industrial revolution. Almost everyone was better off than they were before, better off than anyone could remember being, and the Christian faith had been taken virtually around the world through the great missionary expansion of the Christian faith. But that optimism, that increasingly misplaced faith in the perfectibility and the goodness of human nature, collapsed in the horror of World War I.

Karl Barth has described how the optimism of the reigning liberalism of the age was drowned out by the guns that destroyed a generation of European youth. Then, before humanity had time to take a deep breath, we were visited by a monstrous evil that sprang from what was, by most measures, the most scientifically, educationally, medically, technologically advanced society in the world—Germany.

What happened in that society, the Third Reich, between 1933 and 1945 was something so evil that we have not been able fully to rid ourselves of the ghastly pall cast by its evil shadow. It shattered the optimism of modern man, or it should have, and it reminded us that education, science, and cultural sophistication and advancement do not inoculate us against the evil that lurks within. And what happened in Germany could not have happened in the Germany of Martin Luther. It awaited a leadership that had taken away the German people's confidence in Luther and Luther's God so that there was only a minority of those blessed saints called "the Confessing Church" that as early as 1934 saw evil, knew it when they saw it, and spoke unflinchingly against it.

In 1949 the Nobel Laureate, T. S. Eliot, warned of the West's inevitable choice between a reassertion of Judeo-Christian values in culture or acquiescence to an emerging pagan humanistic culture that worshiped itself.[1] Aleksandr Solzhenitsyn, one of the twentieth century's greatest and bravest men, warned of the dangers of this humanistic thinking of ourselves more highly than we ought to think. In 1978 Solzhenitsyn delivered Harvard University's commencement address, in which he warned America of the grievous consequences of this fallacious, humanistic worldview: "The humanistic way of thinking, which has proclaimed itself our guide, did not admit the existence of intrinsic evil in man, nor did it see any task higher than the attainment of happiness on earth. It started modern Western civilization on the dangerous trend of worshipping man and his material needs . . . as if human life did not have any higher meaning."[2]

Dr. Martin Luther King Jr., another Nobel recipient, understood the depth of evil, both without and within, that confronted him, and he understood the insufficiency of mere human power and reason to conquer it. He told his people in 1963, "The humanist hope is an illusion."[3]

In his book *The Naked Public Square*, Richard John Neuhaus recounts an incident that illustrates the point I am seeking to make. Quite soon after Dr. King's assassination in April 1968, an ecumenical memorial service took place in Harlem. Neuhaus tells how television covered the event.

The announcer . . . spoke in solemn tones:

"And so today there was a memorial service for the slain civil rights leader, Dr. Martin Luther King, Jr. It was a religious service for the slain civil rights leader, Dr. Martin Luther King, Jr. It was a religious service, and it is fitting that it should be, for, after all, Dr. King was the son of a minister."

How to explain this astonishing blindness to the religious motive and meaning of Dr. King's ministry? The announcer was speaking out of a habit of mind that was no doubt quite unconscious. The habit of mind is that religion must be kept at one remove from the public square, that matters of public significance must be sanitized of all religious particularity. It regularly occurred that the klieg lights for the television cameras would be turned off during Dr. King's speeches when he dwelt on the religious and moral-philosophical basis of the movement for racial justice. They would be turned on again when the subject touched upon confrontational politics. In a luncheon conversation Dr. King once remarked, "They aren't interested in the why of what we're doing, only in the what of what we're doing, and because they don't understand the why, they cannot really understand the what."[4]

Newscasters and social analysts like these are not part of any conscious conspiracy against the religious, but they are "victims of a secularizing mythology of which they are hardly aware."[5] And as President Kennedy reminded us, "The great enemy of truth is very often not a lie, deliberate, contrived and dishonest, but the myth, persistent, persuasive and unrealistic."[6]

The fact that racism is at its foundation a spiritual problem and will be vanquished ultimately only by spiritual means does not mean that legislative and judicial remedies should not be, must not be, applied to racial discrimination and bigotry. Another myth that must be challenged is the belief that "you can't legislate morality." Actually, to a very significant degree, society can, and it must. As New Testament Christians, we believe the most sustained statement in the Bible concerning the role of the divinely appointed civil magistrate is in Romans, and it says God ordained civil magistrates to punish those who do evil and reward those who do what is right (Rom. 13:1–8). If you take away from the government the authority and the ability to do that, you have taken away from government the primary reason God gave us government.

Laws against murder, laws against theft, laws against rape, and laws against racism are the legislation of morality. And when we pass laws making murder, theft, rape, and racism illegal, we are not so much trying to impose our morality on murderers, thieves, rapists, and racists as much as we are trying to keep them from imposing their immorality on their victims. Murder, theft, rape, and racism are by definition not between consenting adults in private.

Racial discrimination furnishes an excellent example of this principle. Legislative and judicial remedies radically altered the status of *de jure* segregation and legally institutionalized racial discrimination in our society. Some of us in this audience, if you were in a particular time and place, are old enough to remember and to have experienced the dramatic differences between then and now. I am just old enough to have been in on the very end of legalized, institutional segregation. I can remember segregated buses as a young boy. I can remember segregated waiting rooms and water fountains. Born in 1946, the first year of the baby boom, I grew up in Houston, Texas, a city with approximately 25 percent African-American population. And yet the racial segregation in which I grew up was so rigid that the first

African American my own age that I ever knew, I met when I was a Princeton University freshman.

Oh, I was always taught at home—and I thank God for this—that racism was wrong, and that not only was it wrong, it was sinful. It was against the teaching of Jesus to treat anyone as less than yourself because of the color of his or her skin. Still, I went to a segregated school, I lived in a segregated neighborhood, I worshiped in a segregated church.

So, I went off to Princeton in the fall of 1965 and learned that one of my suite mates was an African American from New Orleans. We soon discovered we had more in common with each other than anyone else in the dormitory. We were the only southerners in the dorm. First, we both nearly froze to death. Second, we couldn't figure out what they were feeding us in the dining hall. Third, we were the only two folks there who didn't have an accent.

Yet, when the law was changed as a result of the prophetic witness of Christians and ministers like Dr. King, black and white, northern and southern, the South changed. You don't think the law made a difference? In the census of 1970, the South was the most segregated region of America in terms of housing and enrollment patterns. In the 1990 census, twenty years later, the South had become the most integrated part of the nation in terms of those same patterns of measurement. One of the primary reasons was that those civil rights laws applied more directly to the South than to any other part of the country because southern societal practices revealed massive evidence of widespread patterns of systemic discrimination.

What about when we move beyond the law? What about *de facto* segregation and discrimination? Here you are dealing with attitudes, not actions. When you enter the realm of the mind, and of the heart, you are moving beyond the power of restraint. If elimination, not restraint, of racial prejudice and bigotry is the goal—and as Christians it must be—then we must move beyond legislative and judicial answers to spiritual answers. However, belief in the necessity of the latter does not eliminate the need for, or our obligation to support, the former.

I want to share with you a sermon that was delivered April 19, 1961, in the chapel at the Southern Baptist Theological Seminary in Louisville, Kentucky. It was delivered by a thirty-two-year-old newly graduated Ph.D. who was the copastor with his illustrious father of the Ebenezer Baptist Church in Atlanta, namely Martin Luther King, Jr. He spoke of the winds of change and of the church's opportunity and responsibility on the frontiers of racial tension. He said, "We are broken loose from the Egypt of slavery; we have moved through the wilderness of segregation; we stand on the border of the Promised Land of integration." If with profound humility I could extend Dr. King's biblical progression, I would note with great sadness almost four decades later we still await the kingdom of racial reconciliation.

Dr. King said directly that racism was a moral issue and had to be confronted by the churches as such. He said somebody must have "sense enough to resist physical force with soul force, to resist hatred with love, and to do so non-violently."

He then went from chapel to speak to the ethics students from all the ethics classes at the seminary. So many other students wanted to leave their classes and come to hear him lecture that they finally went from a larger hall to a larger hall, and then they ended up in chapel, which was the only building on campus large enough to house all the students who wanted to hear Dr. King's lecture. Over five hundred students were in attendance at that noon-hour luncheon. He spoke about the need for the church to confront its past, to confront the fact that the most segregated moment in American life is when we gather to worship God on Sunday morning.[7]

That is still true and one reason it is true is because that's the most voluntary moment in American social life. We are free to do and to worship where we want to worship and with whom we want to worship, and we segregate ourselves so that it is the most racially divided moment in any point in our week. The point Dr. King was attempting to make—and the one I am trying to make as well—is that the law changed a lot of things. Those things needed to be changed and they would not have changed without the law being on the right side. However, while the salt of the law can change actions, it is only the light of the gospel that can change attitudes. The salt of the law can change behaviors, but it is only the light of the gospel that can change beliefs. The salt of the law can change habits, but it is only the light of the gospel that can change hearts.

We have got the only answer as Christians to the sin nature that makes us think more highly of ourselves than we ought to think, which is the foundational core of racism. That sin nature entices us and seduces us into making gaps and distances between ourselves and those who are different from us.

One more myth must be addressed at this point. It is a prevalent myth in America, and it is one against which we ought to be able to give eloquent testimony. That is the myth that the people who are the objects of racial prejudice are the only victims. Many of us know from personal experience the falsehood of that myth. All of us, perpetrators and victims alike, are shackled by the chains of prejudice—it victimizes everyone.

As a Princeton sophomore, I took a course on racism in American culture. As part of that course's assignment, I read a book, *Killers of the Dream*, by Lillian Smith, a native Georgian who finally left the South in despair at midcentury. In *Killers of the Dream* Lillian Smith writes with breathtaking and broken-hearted pathos of her Georgia girlhood experience of this joint victimization. Recognizing that she penned these words in 1949,

I trust you will accept her heartfelt words and forgive her dated ethnic terminology:

> The mother who taught me what I know of tenderness and love and compassion taught me also the bleak rituals of keeping Negroes in their "place." The father who rebuked me for an air of superiority toward schoolmates from the mill and rounded out his rebuke by gravely reminding me that "all men are brothers," trained me in the steel-rigid decorums I must demand of every colored male. . . .
>
> So we learned the dance that cripples the human spirit, step by step by step, we who were white and we who were colored, day by day, hour by hour, year by year until the movements were reflexes and made for the rest of our lives without thinking. . . .
>
> Something was wrong with a world that tells you that love is good and people are important and then forces you to deny love and to humiliate people. . . . in trying to shut the Negro race away from us, we have shut ourselves away from so many good, creative, honest, deeply human things in life. . . . the warped, distorted form we have put around every Negro child from birth is around every white child also. Each is on a different side of the frame but each is pinioned there. . . . what cruelly shapes and cripples the personality of one is as cruelly shaping and crippling the personality of the other.[8]

Everyone is victimized when bigotry and racism occur—the oppressor and the oppressed—perhaps the oppressor more than the oppressed, because they have to deal with the guilt of what they intuitively know—from the law written on the conscience—to be wrong (Rom. 2:15).

When I shared Lillian Smith's quote with my trustees a few years ago, a trustee approached me after the session with tears streaming down her face. She said, "When I was a little girl, about ten years old, I went downtown to have lunch with my father. I got on the bus and the white section of the bus was full. An adult white male got up and told a black woman to get up so I could sit down. I can't tell you the anguish and shame I felt," she said. "I had always been taught to do what adults told me to do, but there was something in me that knew that was terribly, terribly wrong. The pain of that has stayed with me to this day." How many millions of times did that happen; and every time that it happened, it shriveled and shrunk the soul and the spirit of the oppressor, perhaps more even than the oppressed.

Lillian Smith despaired of the victims ever completely overcoming such a formative, or should we say "de-formative," experience. Even when they summoned the strength and knowledge to escape the frame, she viewed them and herself as "stunted and warped and in our lifetime cannot grow straight again."[9] Happily, Lillian Smith was wrong.

In Christ Jesus we can be made new. In Christ we can be healed and liberated from our past. In Christ we can start over with our past and we can start over with our dreams. Paul tells us that we "can do all things through Christ which strengtheneth me" (Phil. 4:13). Victimizer and victim alike find liberation from their victimization in Jesus Christ. Many of us have seen this change with our own eyes. Some here tonight have experienced it personally. People who internalized this racism in all of its spiritual virulence have, in Christ, overcome it and been truly changed.

I remember vividly the moment when the moral and theological insufficiency of mere passive belief in racial equality crystallized for me—a postwar baby boomer, raised in a rigidly segregated society. This was the moment when I understood my responsibility never to tolerate, but to challenge racism, whenever and wherever I encountered it. I was sixteen years old, sitting in my living room in Houston, Texas, watching the evening news, August 28, 1963. Suddenly, extraordinary television images flickered across the screen. People, tens of thousands of people, filled the expanse between the Lincoln and Washington memorials.

Then a voice rolled across the scene with soaring, eloquent words of hope and of conviction and Dr. King said:

> . . . even though we face the difficulties of today and tomorrow, I still have a dream. It is a dream deeply rooted in the American dream.
>
> I have a dream that one day this nation will rise up and live out the true meaning of its creed: "We hold these truths to be self-evident; that all men are created equal." I have a dream that one day on the red hills of Georgia the sons of former slaves and sons of former slave owners will be able to sit down together at the table of brotherhood.
>
> I have a dream that my four little children will one day live in a nation where they will not be judged by the color of their skin but by the content of their character.

I must pause at this point to note that Dr. King's dream was not a secular, but a moral dream, which envisioned discernments and judgments made according to "character," not "color."

Dr. King continued his elegant oration:

> This is our hope. This is the faith that I go back to the South with. With this faith we will be able to hew out of the mountain of despair a stone of hope. With this faith we will be able to transform the jangling discords of our nation into a beautiful symphony of Brotherhood. . . .
>
> This will be the day when all of God's children will be able to sing with new meaning, "My country 'tis of thee, sweet land of liberty, of thee I sing: Land

where my fathers died, land of the Pilgrims' pride,
from every mountainside, let freedom ring."[10]

Words to confront and penetrate the Christian spirit and convict the American soul. Why should I not have been convinced, captivated, convicted? And I was. For what was Dr. King doing but appealing to the truth I had imbibed in Sunday school?

Red and yellow, black and white,
They are precious in His sight.
Jesus loves the little children of the world.

What was Dr. King doing but focusing attention on the pledge that I took each morning of every school day in my segregated school?

I pledge allegiance to the flag of the United States of America and to the Republic for which it stands, one Nation under God, indivisible, with liberty and justice for all.

What was Dr. King doing but appealing to the fulfillment of the promise of our national documents such as the Declaration of Independence?

We hold these truths to be self-evident, that all men are created equal, that they are endowed by their Creator with certain unalienable Rights, that among these are Life, Liberty, and the pursuit of Happiness.

The Declaration's author, Thomas Jefferson, understood the principle's unfulfilled promise. Jefferson's troubled words regarding the glaring disparity between the nation's promise and the nation's practice, *his* promise and *his* practice, are chiseled into the wall of Jefferson's memorial in our nation's capital:

Can the Liberties of a Nation be secure when we
have removed a conviction that these liberties are the
gifts of God? Indeed I tremble for my country when
I reflect that God is just, that his justice cannot sleep
forever. Commerce between master and slave is des-
potism. Nothing is more certainly written in the
book of fate than that these people are to be free.

In our resolve to go forward, to do more, we should pause to
take inspiration from the progress that has been made. It has not
been enough. It has been woefully inadequate, but there has been
change. We need to draw courage from that change to move from
standing on the border of the promised land of integration, to
moving forward to the kingdom of reconciliation. It will not happen without a faithful Christian witness. We have failed too often
in the past in America. We have had two great religious awaken-
ings and slavery survived both, because we did not understand
adequately the need to move from our personal lives to our
prophetic commission to be salt and light in our society.

Jesus *commanded* us to be salt. He *commanded* us to be light.
Salt has to touch that which it would preserve and come into
contact with that which it would purify. Jesus commanded us to
be salt and light. A Christianity that has lost its vertical vision
has lost its salt. But a Christianity that forgets its horizontal
commission to be ambassadors of reconciliation has forgotten
the Incarnation, the Word made flesh that "dwelt among us"
(John 1:14). Racism is a global problem and it has a global solution. That solution's hope is found in the cross of our Savior.
Now, I'm not talking about a merely pietistic, "let's just change
hearts." We have to call for racial justice and we must live racial
justice and racial reconciliation. And those who have been identified as the oppressors have a special burden to reach out again,
and again, and again to those they have historically pushed away
and shunted aside.

As one African-American Southern-Baptist pastor said to me when we got to know each other well enough that we could be honest, "Richard, you've got to understand that you white people are a very complicated people. You don't always mean what you say, and you don't always say what you mean." That observation needed no explanation.

Some people see things the way they are and say "Why?" Others dream dreams that never were and say "Why not?" Let's identify with men and women like Dr. King who saw visions that never were—who dreamed dreams that never have been—of a society in which we are judged not by the color of our skin but by the content of our character.

An old African proverb says, "Tell me and I'll listen; show me and I'll believe." This is what we must do. We must allow God to change our minds and our hearts until our actions are transformed. We must show the world we really believe what we say we believe, and that God will really do what we say he will do.

We must pray that God will give us passion as well as compassion. We must call upon Baptists and other Christians to resolve to stand publicly and privately for racial reconciliation and justice and to speak out against racism whenever and wherever we encounter it.

We must as individuals, as families, as communities of worship reach across racial boundaries to establish friendships, through meal times, prayer times, and recreational times.

We must call upon Baptists and other Christians to apologize for past bigotry and to pray for, and minister to, those still within its deadly clutches, either as persecuted or as persecutor.

As a Southern Baptist I call upon my fellow Southern Baptists, out of our own incessant past experience, and intermittent present experience with racism, to witness both near and far to racism's devastating and debilitating impact on all its victims, persecuted and persecutor.

Chapter 3

Don't Let Skin Stop You!

N. SPENCER GLOVER
Jeremiah 13:23a

The time has come when, in the family of Christians, pretension must give way to sanctified sincerity. It's time that we seriously understood that "color scheme" was not a mistake of the Creator in his calling forth of the botanical and zoological kingdoms, nor in his making of humanity. God did nothing without purpose, and that includes "color scheme."

Problems always arise when humanity sets up its own purposes and they run counter to God's. It is then that we resort to creating our own gods that we can move about and change at will to suit our own purposes. This brings about the supreme necessity of clearing the air,

---

N. SPENCER GLOVER is pastor of Trinity Missionary Baptist Church in Cincinnati, Ohio, a congregation he has served for more than twenty years. As an undergraduate, he majored in music at the Pierre-Royston Academy of Arts in New York, later pursuing graduate studies in theology at International Bible Institute and Seminary, Trinity Lutheran Theological School, Josephinum Pontifical College in Ohio, and Princeton Theological Seminary. He serves as professor of theology at Temple Bible College and Seminary of Cincinnati and has been a visiting lecturer at the Southern Baptist Theological Seminary in Louisville. An outstanding preacher, educator, and community activist, Dr. Glover has an abiding commitment to racial reconciliation and has influenced several generations of younger ministers through his passion, wisdom, and ability to reach out across racial and denominational lines.

when we hear the title *God* used, asking: What *God?* If we are talking about the Judeo-Christian God, the God of Abraham, Isaac, and Jacob, and the inimitable Father of Jesus, the God of the Bible, that fact regulates our thinking on everything.

If we are professing Christians, the very cruciality of the idea of racism should send us to the Scripture in search of a word from God. Is racism a word he recognizes, or is it a term that humanity has placed in the shadow of the Almighty with the hope that it would be baptized with his righteousness?

When we look at the meaning of racism and see that it is an exaggeration of inherent racial differences and a prejudice in favor of certain races, grading them in terms of *superiority* of one to another, it doesn't fit with the God of the Bible. Humanity has superimposed this system, first on itself and then on God.

I have to say it this way, because in the text I have chosen, God sets forth his position on the matter, in the form of a rhetorical question: "Can the Ethiopian change his skin, or the leopard his spots?" (Jer. 13:23a). You don't have to engage in deep thought to see that the question requires a *no* answer, and that answer is expected. That answer, however, cannot just be shouted out, without examining the implications it suggests.

In case there are among my readers some experts in hermeneutics, I need to say that I am not lifting the text out of context, for you will see as you read on that strong implications from the text are suggested there. The context suggests that the people of Jerusalem are being exposed and stripped for a host of sins. The people have become so taken over by their corrupt behavior that it has them hopelessly fixed in it. They can no more change their ways than an Ethiopian could change his skin or a leopard his spots.

The Ethiopian's skin suggests race as indicated by *color*—the leopard's spots suggest *color* and the color implied is black. Lurking behind the question is the possible response: if they could, they would change the skin color and the spot color that make possible their identification. No, they cannot remove the black color. It's a divine, creative gift that has to do with God's eternal purpose. No, they cannot remove the black color. They didn't give it. They can't take it away. It's skin. It's not the person. It's not the leopard. It's skin. It's covering, but I suggest to you that our racism begins in skin.

The text asks the question about skin change, which is the first noticeable indication of race, but to mistake *indication* for *essence* is the root of racism. It makes *color* a characteristic of personality and pronounces a false judgment on morality and sends out biographical error on people of color.

The fact that God raises the race question in the text is a signal for the necessity of asking: Why cannot an Ethiopian change his skin? Why would he want to? The first question calls us to realize that *color scheme* is God-willed. In the science of color, black is basic; other colors come out of it and can be returned to it. Now when we note that in the Genesis creation story, God makes man from the dust of the earth, he had to be very dark, because only rich, dark earth could have brought forth the botanical kingdom.

We must further understand that the area called the Garden of Eden, where man was placed, was geographically northeast in the land called not Africa, but Ethiopia. Therefore, God asks Jeremiah: Can an Ethiopian change his skin? Can one whose ancestry is in this land change his skin? The question, Why would he want to? is more complicated because those of us of Ethiopian, African- or Afro-Asiatic ancestry have been traditionally exposed to Eurocentric Bible interpreters, who have tried to eliminate the Afro-Asiatic from the groups and label them nonblacks. However, if you are a United States Bible reader, this gives you an additional *skin* problem, because it is still on record that a minuscule amount of traceable black blood classifies you as black. For this reason I couldn't be shocked when my blond and blue-eyed seminary professor announced to our class that, under the law, he was black.

Black is basic, uneraseable, unchangeable, but not the product of a curse; it cannot be changed. Biblical geography makes clear that races are intentional and have divinely intentional roles on the master plan of him who doeth all things well. To allow racism to cause us to decide against being who and what we are makes living in this world one big problem.

If we believe that the Bible teaches black skin to be a curse, then we must also believe white skin to be a curse. Read carefully Genesis 9, and you will see that Canaan, Ham's son, was cursed to be a "servant of servants . . . unto his brethren." Note that Noah, his grandfather, cursed him—not God. Read also 2 Kings 5, and see that Gehazi, the servant of Elisha, was cursed with the leprosy from which Naaman had been healed because he disobeyed the prophet. Verse 27 says, "The leprosy therefore of Naaman shall cleave unto thee, and unto thy seed for ever. And he went out from his presence a leper as white as snow." I believe you can see from these quotes that they are open to speculation, and the answer derived depends upon who is doing the speculating.

However, to give heed to the testimony of nature is to understand that "color scheme" has purpose in the overall plan of God. It has to do with climate, survival, beauty, and comeliness, but it was never intended to promote separation and estrangement. Diversity, yes, but estrangement, no. The reality of God's human creation is "out of one blood, God made all nations to dwell upon the earth" (Acts 17:26)—not out of one skin. But skin color in America has caused much disruption because of estrangement as if color will rub off; that's not a laughing matter.

I recall my wife coming home from her high school teaching assignment, down in spirit, and telling me that her day had been spoiled, because in speaking to a white student she had touched his arm and he snatched his arm back and jumped back. She walked out of the room to the principal's office and rubbed him on the arm and asked, "Do I rub off on you?" The principal knew immediately what had happened. The student was removed from my wife's class and given a schedule change. Say what you will, that's a distorted view of reality. The view is only "skin deep." Can the Ethiopian change his skin or the leopard change its spots? If they could, why should they?

Prejudgment on the basis of color results in the distortion of reality and sends us false signals announcing white as superior to black and, in some cases, black as superior to white. These present misreadings of the signals keep the melting pot that is America "boiling," because governmental decisions, at all levels, are made mainly on the basis of race.

But let us not dwell too long on politics, because all the guilt is not there. Some of the tentacles of racism have reached into the church of God. The questions have to be raised: Does the church care? Does the clergy? It's a shame to have to say it, but we must speak the truth. The church in America has been silent a long time on the issue of racism. Instead of being destroyers of the serpent, we have warmed and nurtured him and given him a home. Many black and white churchgoers stop at the point of toleration and haven't gone any deeper. Racial reconciliation scares us off.

Toleration does not necessarily admit a historical and biographical relationship. It rather admits a possibility of "putting up with" visible skin differences. But it does not go far enough to say that we are all related. The "one blood" tie of all nations that dwell upon the face of the earth is deeper than visible skin. We are all ancestrally connected. The Bible tells us we are geographically connected and religiously connected.

If you are deeply interested, study Genesis 2, geographically and Genesis 10, biographically. Turn to Acts 8, and be enlightened by the race of the Ethiopian eunuch, which should lead you to check on Philip, his chariot companion, who you can discover to have been dark in skin color. Keep reading and you will come upon the men of Cyprus and Cyrene who carried the gospel from Jerusalem to Antioch. Geographically, they were men of dark hue. I'm simply calling to your attention the necessity of not dismissing a biblical testimony: "out of one blood" all nations were created.

Now, all of the foregoing suggests that before accepting racism as our religion, we need to do more than *see* the skin. We need to *think under* the skin where the real person dwells. There is no color of spirit that is housed in flesh. Soul has no hue. All blood is red. All hearts pump red blood throughout the veins and arteries. Blood is the life. Somewhere in the midst of veins and arteries, capillaries, ligaments, and muscles dwells the soul, which God saves by his grace and reconciles to himself. This is the real person, which is covered by skin. We need to see through the "house" to the living spirit, which is colorless, untouchable, but REAL.

I believe that racial reconciliation must happen in the inner man before it can be lived out visibly by the outer man. There must be in us an overcoming of the estrangement between humankind and God on the matter of our racism. God never intended separatism from anything but sin, and we need to stop "twisting" Scripture to make him say it. Everyone guilty of this must confess, "It's me, it's me, O Lord." Since separatism is not God's intention, he cannot bless where his will is denied. So we must openly and fully take our own blame.

We cannot expect government, constitutions, amendments, written or unwritten laws to correct this matter. We must understand that racism is a matter of relations between God and man; and man and man; therefore, it is on God's judgment docket. We must further recognize that, on this matter, we are enemies of God because we are opposed to his will.

Black and white believers must be constrained by the love of God to take part, without obstruction, in the faith common to Christians, and there are no "separate-but-equal" arrangements in this. White congregations building megachurch buildings in the suburbs and selling or "donating" worn-out buildings in the inner city to black congregations—thus promoting white religious flight—are dodging reconciliation.

However, there is a "back draft" to this action that tends to move the black church into the will of God. The slighting, the coldness toward interracial couples and families send them to the black church where they are warmly received, integrated into the fellowship, and warmly accepted. It is Christian for the black community to call upon white professing brothers and sisters to practice all that being a Christian means, especially all that is involved in overcoming the estrangement. We must mainly consider that the estrangement is two-pronged; therefore, the reconciliation is two-pronged.

First, it is reconciliation to God through Christ, for it is Christ who does the "bringing together" that is the action energy of the term "to reconcile." Man is first reconciled to God, which is an "under-the-skin" happening. It's an operation of the Spirit of God (colorless) upon the spirit of man (colorless) revealing the love of God, as expressed on the cross, to the heart of man (spiritual), which at the time is "ungodly," weak, and as Romans 5:10 says, "enemies" of God.

The word *enemy* has built into it the absence of "peace." No peace between man and God causes enmity between man and man, and this widens the distance between man and God. Somebody has to move, and the movement must be in two directions—man to God and man to man.

This two-faceted movement cannot be disjointed and that is what we, both black and white, fail to understand. There can be no reconciliation with God apart from reconciliation with man. That's why the apostle Paul announces in 2 Corinthians 5:19, "In Christ God was reconciling the world (of mankind) to himself" (NRSV). Christ is the hinge that holds the two facets together. Thus, the hymnologist was right when he wrote: "In Christ there is no East nor West, in Him no South or North, but one great fellowship of love throughout the whole wide earth." In such fellowship, the Ethiopian has no call to change his color, nor the leopard to change his spots, for Christ reconciles him, color and all, to God and to all persons. It's an "under-the-skin" happening that works out through the skin.

This being the case, why is it that we consistently give a voice to the unchangeable skin and drown out the "still small voice" from under the skin. African Americans must refuse to mess with their divinely given genetics systems and stop trying to cover their effects. There is no harm in wearing the outer display of Ethiopia. It's only skin deep. Cosmetic camouflages only last between showers and baths. *It washes off.* Face lifting, nose paring, skin bleaching only effect epidermis, but *underneath* it is soul territory, the *real* you and me. Can an Ethiopian really change his skin? Remember that "cover up" *is not change.*

Let me switch the analogy for a moment. If black and its derivatives are so undesirable, then why are there so many cruise ships and air flights bound to the Caribbean, where white people lie in the sun and pick up some degree of blackness, even knowing the risk of skin cancer? There must be something beautiful about it, something attractive and something desirable. Only racism has a negative view of blackness. But when Christ is allowed to work the grace of reconciliation "under the skin," the view from outside has no effect on the truth from inside. Don't let skin stop you from listening to the still small voice from "under the skin." Its origin is from the soul, which is colorless.

I think I hear a question coming from the Christian community. Can we not consider ourselves reconciled when in our church conventions and hierarchy conclaves we have declared in writing that we will work toward color blindness? I ask you, have you not noticed how difficult it is to stand in blowing dust and keep from getting specks in your eyes? Likewise, it is difficult to stand in the midst of resolutions to do right, to be the defenders of reconciliation, while the winds of racism keep blowing trash in our eyes.

Never forget that we, the reconcilers black and white, are at war with principalities and powers in high places. An active element of strength in American life is the racism in the air. It influences politics, institutional functions, against which the Christian community has not yet publicly and nationally declared *all-out* war. The reconciling church must not only declare but live out the unabridged, soul-transforming Word of God, which has the facility to pick out the racist trash from our eyes. Recommendations without *living ratification* won't make real reconcilers.

The church—black, whit, and "other"—must declare racism a common enemy opposed to the oneness of the family of God. God has no stepchildren! Therefore, if we identify with God as our Father, we must become reconciled as full brothers and sisters, living witnesses of one church family under God. In our kind of world this is risky business, but a Christian church should not refuse to accept risks; this is a misnomer. The genuine color-blind church will be at risk of losing its "as-is-ness," but will gain the spiritual power inherent in reconciliation.

Inherent spiritual power, resident in reconciliation and bestowed upon the receivers, is the power to shatter anxious self-centeredness, which is the preserver of racism. When the

Christian church surrenders to the authority of Christ, the delusion that it can keep itself is shattered. The membership begins to understand that self-preservation is the real enemy and that they need to be rescued from its grasp and only God can give the help they need. Only he can do the shattering and reconcile them to himself and to one another. Inviting God to shatter anxious self-centeredness opens the way for reconciliation to occur. God is now free to make real in us the testimony of Galatians 2:19b–20: "I have been crucified with Christ; and it is no longer I who live, but it is Christ who lives in me. And the life I now live in the flesh I live by faith in the Son of God, who loved me and gave himself for me" (NRSV).

I am sure that Paul would not mind our taking these, his words, as a creedal statement of the reconciled. The old racist self has been crucified with Christ. The "I" that it represented no longer lives, but Christ—with no racist ties, no color allegiances—lives in me and through me so that the flesh in which I live, though it be black, red, yellow, or white, I live by faith in the Son of God who loves me as his brother/sister, and gave himself for me, to reconcile me to our Father and to every other person who calls him Father.

It's not a matter of what color we are, or what nationality, or what language we speak, but whether we are true beings in right relation with God. This puts us in right relation with each other. That means that the oneness of the family of God makes us blood kin, for it is the blood of Jesus that cleanses us from all unrighteousness—and that "all" includes racism. To be reconciled to God through the blood of Christ binds us to the "in Christ" emphasis of the apostle Paul.

Being "in Christ" was, for Paul, the center and soul of Christian experience. He considered it the essence of the Christian life. Basically, the term "in Christ" describes a spiritual relationship, which is not confined by space and time. It is an unlimited relationship with the risen Lord. Under the "in Christ" theme, all Christians are the children of God by faith in Christ Jesus, as stated in Galatians 5–6. An important element of this theme is that it can never be guilty of disunity because every Christian is in Christ and there can never be any barrier between those who are truly Christian.

How can professed Christians, of whatever color, raise barriers of racism between themselves as churches or individuals? Christianity does not mean being in a church, but being *in Christ*. A Christian's whole life will be in Christ. Thank God, we have the opportunity to enter into a relationship with Christ in which our whole life will be in Christ. We can genuinely experience a thoroughgoing reconciliation with God and man. *Don't Let Skin Stop You!*

I said early on that the text raised a rhetorical question that required the answer *no*. We cannot change our color. We can "mix" it, mask it, tan it, but we can never change it at the root. Cosmetology, scientific gadgeting, or mere wishing will never make it so. Neither will racist vocabulary or political schema. God does not intend change of skin, but he does intend that skin not stop us from unifying as one family in Christ. Now, it's no surprise to God that human beings object to that. They oppose the reconciled life because it means that there can be no unreconciled life that is in Christ.

Life in Christ involves self-surrender in which the racist self is transformed from a hostile, fearful, and anxious self to a secure life in the love of God. The life in Christ is one in which the selfish ego dies. There is a turning away from self-aggrandizement to the truth that there are other selves God loves as he loves us and they must see the living, loving, life-changing Christ in me.

The reconciled life is a life freed from self-seeking because its power *to be* is rooted in the grace of God. The sovereign grace of God alone gives, empowers, and brings to manifestation the act of reconciliation. Reconciliation is really what the life, death, and resurrection of Jesus the Christ is about. Reconciliation is the unconditional acceptance by God of undeserving people like you and me. Reconciliation is, therefore, an act under sovereign grace wherein God offers us no condemnation and freedom from neurotic dependence on and approval of others.

Saving and delivering grace has its existence in the love of God, for the apostle John tells us, "God is Love." So, out of "God's is-ness," his love is made manifest in sovereign grace, which permits us to be reconciled to him and stand in his love. The reconciled life loves with the very kind of love with which it has been loved, and this love is seasoned with grace. That seasoning is more than pleasing taste. Like salt, it also has a preserving function. As salt draws out destructive water, so love seasoned with grace draws out of the reconciled life all hatred, fear, and anxious self-centeredness.

With these destructives drawn from us, the racist self is transformed and we stand firm and secure in the love that God is; and we come to know the fullness of being in the family of God. We are not reconciled from the outside in, but from the inside out. Therefore, the Ethiopian's skin and the leopard's spots need not change anywhere but in our concepts.

Much is being said today about self-esteem and self-affirmation, but remember that the reconciled life finds a new form of self-affirmation. It is a transformed life wherein we are reconciled to both God and man. Racism is full of the will to power and glory. That glory is pure self-glory. It lifts one human being above another because of creed and color, and that's racism. But Christian self-esteem or self-affirmation is loving ourselves as a gift from God. A gift is not to be kept but surrendered to God, to be used according to his purposes. Instead of striving to climb on and over one another, we lose ourselves in dedication of our lives to God. I hear somebody saying, "That's wiping self out." Not really; that's simply recognizing that the "old person" has been crucified with Christ. The damnable ego has died, and the sanctified ego has been resurrected.

Reconciliation declares to us that in Christ the pride of racism is overcome. A person who is reconciled to God has a new and clear vision of the distance between himself or herself and God. He or she is very clear about his or her frailty and dependence upon him. The arrogance, the feeling of total independence, and the thought of self-sufficiency that kept them puffed-up have now been transformed. In comparison to what they were, the racists now "hunger and thirst" after righteousness, which can come only by the empowerment of grace.

When we are transformed by the power of grace, we know that there is no level of life at which man holds within himself his own fulfillment. We can only copy with thanksgiving the words of the apostle Paul: "By the grace of God I am what I am" (1 Cor. 15:10).

Can the Ethiopian change his skin? No, by the grace of God he is what he is. Can the Asian—can the African American—can the Caucasian—change his skin? No, by the grace of God they are what they are. I invite you, though, to get under the skin—where it really counts—and see that the inner man is in no way different from you. Learn to thank God for *sameness.*

Chapter 4

The Answer to Racial Discrimination

STEPHEN F. OLFORD

Acts 17:16–34; James 2:1–12; Romans 10:1–12

In 1959 I accepted the call of God to be senior minister of the Calvary Baptist Church in New York City. It never occurred to me to raise the question of racism in a church in metropolitan New York—with all its mix of nationalities! In fact, the issue was never mentioned in the negotiations that were transacted between New York and London—where I was pastor of the Duke Street Baptist Church in Richmond, Surrey. Perhaps I assumed too much when making inquiries about the new pastoral charge. But to say the least, I was more than dismayed to discover that Calvary Baptist Church had a segregated membership.

One thing was clear. The situation had to change if I

STEPHEN F. OLFORD is founder and senior lecturer of the Stephen Olford Center for Biblical Preaching. Dr. Olford served as minister of Duke Street Baptist Church in Richmond, Surrey, England (1953–1959) and the famed Calvary Baptist Church in New York City (1959–1973). His ministry at Calvary coincided with the Civil Rights Movement in this country. In this context, he led his church to open its doors to persons of all races—a story he recounts in the introduction to this sermon. Dr. Olford now lives in Memphis, Tennessee, where with his son, Dr. David Olford, he promotes biblical preaching and practical training for the Christian ministry. A close friend and colleague of Dr. Billy Graham, Dr. Stephen Olford has traveled the world preaching the Word in many crusades, conventions, and centers of learning. He is the author of many books, including Not I But Christ, The Way of Holiness, and Anointed Expository Preaching.

was to continue as pastor of that congregation. I prayed much about the matter and then began an in-depth study of the problem. I discovered that 85 percent of the church members were against integration.

What made matters worse was the outside pressure that was brought to bear upon me to *act at once*—or else! A black federal judge came to see me, convinced I was a racist. He argued that, since I had not fought the issue to the point of splitting the church, I had proved myself to be a segregationist.

I pleaded with him for patience and explained that the answer to the problem would come through prayer, the preaching of the Word of reconciliation, and the reviving work of the Holy Spirit. Some time later, the judge changed his mind when my secretary made him read one of my sermons on race relations, while he waited for an interview! The interview never took place. The judge studied the manuscript, returned it to my secretary, and said, "I am satisfied!" I never saw him again. As time passed I began to sense a change in the spiritual climate of the church as the message of reconciliation was proclaimed in human weakness, but with the divine authority of God's Word. In fact, such was the moving of the Holy Spirit that the provisional dateline I had set for a church meeting on the race issue was advanced by six months.

I shall never forget that eventful night! "Everybody" was there, including many who should never have been present! I felt it my duty, at this church meeting, to take a *personal* stand and not involve my officers, except as they spoke for themselves.

The sermon I preached was bathed in prayer, and delivered with God-anointed passion. After expounding the Scriptures, I fielded questions. It is true that vitriolic language was used by some, and that tense moments were experienced by all. But when it came to a vote, the tally was practically unanimous. Only eleven people raised their hands in opposition. Of these, seven assured me that while they did not agree with me on this matter, they were prepared to support the ministry and reconsider their "views" on race relations. The remaining four were sovereignly removed from our midst in a manner that brought "great fear . . . upon all the church" (Acts 5:11). One man died that very week!

I have often been asked how things worked out thereafter in the church. My answer is short and simple: God blessed us beyond all our asking or thinking. Even though we had the problems that are common to any inner-city church, the question of integration was not one of them. We found that the people who sought the right hand of fellowship at Calvary were those who were prepared to submit themselves to the disciplined training of our membership classes, accept the standard of ministry, the mode of worship, and the opportunities for service as structured within our church.

In this connection, we had African-American and other minority groups elected to our boards, committees, choir, and similar organizations, all working together for the glory of God. Sometimes I felt that Calvary Baptist Church was a little Pentecost; for every Sunday there were people from many nations under heaven! At our visitors reception we always had a roll call, and it was noted that an *average* of forty different countries across the world were represented in any given worship service.

Praise the Lord, we learned that *integration comes through reconciliation;* and that reconciliation takes place at the foot of the cross when "red, yellow, black, and white" are prepared to be broken and mastered by the constraining love of Christ.

That was forty years ago, and tragically, racial discrimination in the churches of our land is still one of the burning issues of our times. The build-up of these racial tensions seriously affects every aspect of life. To ignore this problem is to fail in our witness, and to imply the impracticality and impotence of the gospel of Christ.

We do well, therefore, to examine what the Bible has to say about the subject. We shall limit ourselves to a threefold answer:

I. The Sociological Answer to Racial Discrimination

"God shows no partiality. But in every nation whoever fears Him and works righteousness is *accepted by Him*" (Acts 10:34–35 NKJV). The apostle Peter uttered these words after his dramatic deliverance from racism (Acts 9:9–16; 10:9–33). Such language was momentous in sweeping away centuries of racial prejudice. What Peter discovered, Jesus displayed in all his dealings with people of diverse backgrounds, such as the woman of Samaria (John 4:7); the Syro-phoenician (Mark 7:26); and the Roman centurion (Matt. 8:5–13). There appeared to be no place for racial distinctions in his experience and ministry. Indeed, he clearly stated: "I have *other* sheep, which are not of this fold; I must bring them also, and they shall hear My voice; and they shall become one flock with one shepherd" (John 10:16 NASB). In attitude and action he corroborated the consistent witness of the Scriptures that God is the Creator and Redeemer of all mankind and is, therefore, "no respect[er] of persons" (Rom. 2:11).

From this line of teaching we may deduce two main considerations:

(1) The Unity of the Human Family

Speaking to the Athenians who boasted of their racial superiority, Paul declared, "[God] has made from one blood every nation of men to dwell on all the face of the earth, and has determined their preappointed times and the boundaries of their dwellings" (Acts 17:26 NKJV). Few words in Paul's theology are more pregnant with significance as they relate to racial discrimination. He states here that the one common origin of humanity is inseparably bound up with the unity of the Godhead.

Dr. Richard N. Longenecker reminds us that "the substance of the Athenian address concerns the nature of God and the responsibility of man." Therefore, "contrary to all pantheistic and polytheistic notions, God is the one, as Paul says, who created the world and everything in it. He is the Lord of heaven and earth (cf. Gen. 14:19, 22). Paul further affirms the oneness of all humans in their creation by the *one God* and their descent from a *common ancestor*"[1] [emphasis mine]. We have no more right to discriminate between nations or races than we have to discriminate between the persons of the Godhead.

In his inscrutable wisdom, God has so determined seasons and appointed habitations that there is a variety and, therefore, a beauty about the different characteristics of the races of the world. The Hebrew concept of God and righteousness, the Greek sense of beauty and wisdom, the Roman idea of law and power, the Teutonic view of truthfulness and discipline, the Celtic way of impulsiveness and courage, and the Negro trait of patience and service have their particular contribution to make to the mosaic of human life.

All local circumstances of soil and climate that influence human characteristics come under the heading of the "boundaries of [man's] dwellings." Thus, even though races can be divided into Caucasian, Mongolian, and Negroid, they are, in fact, united under one supreme Creator and sustainer of the universe. No one can hold this biblical doctrine of our common ancestry and be a racist.

It is not without significance that the principles of the United Nations embody this concept of the unity of the human family. Under the purposes of membership, the charter of the United Nations states that "the primary objective of the United Nations is the maintenance of international peace and security . . . and is dedicated to the development of friendly relations among nations, *based on the principle of equal rights and self-determination of peoples*; to the achievement of international cooperation in solving international problems of an economic, social, cultural, or humanitarian character; and to serve as a central forum for harmonizing the actions of nations in the attainment of these common ends" [emphasis mine].

But with the unity of the human family, there is:

(2) The Unity of the Heavenly Family

"For you are *all* sons of God through faith in Christ Jesus" (Gal. 3:26 NKJV, emphasis mine). Dr. Griffith Thomas reminds us that as the family of God we are "a society of saved sinners." Thus, discrimination is incompatible with what the gospel of Christ teaches. With this in mind, Paul declares: "As many of you as were baptized into Christ have put on Christ. There is neither Jew nor Greek, there is neither slave nor free, there is neither male nor female; for you are all one in Christ Jesus" (Gal. 3:27–28 NKJV). This means that international, cultural, and sociological barriers are swept away when we are baptized into Christ (1 Cor. 12:13). From that moment onwards, we accept one another *not* as Europeans, Africans, Orientals and so on, but as Christians.

This glorious fact reminds me of the charming African American who requested membership at a certain church some while ago. When refused, he stood aghast and exclaimed, "I wasn't applying as a Negro. I was coming as a Christian."

So there is a sociological answer to this problem of racial discrimination. But there is also:

II. The Nomological Answer to Racial Discrimination

"If you really fulfill the royal law according to the Scripture, 'You shall love your neighbor as yourself,' you do well; but if you show partiality, you commit sin, and are convicted by the law as transgressors. For whoever shall keep the whole law, and yet stumble in one point, he is guilty of all" (James 2:8–10 NKJV). Nomology is the study of the law; and since the law, in the highest meaning of that term, has a biblical foundation, we need to examine what the Scriptures have to say. For our limited purpose, we shall examine one of the most explicit passages on this subject found in the Word of God, James 2:1–12. The apostle James tells us in these verses that racial or social discrimination constitutes a serious violation of the "royal law" that reads, "You shall love your neighbor as yourself" (v. 8). The royal law involves spiritual, social, and civil behavior; therefore, discrimination is:

(1) The Violation of a Spiritual Law

"Listen, my beloved brethren: Has God not chosen the poor of this world to be rich in faith and heirs of the kingdom which He promised to those who love Him? But you have dishonored the poor man. Do not the rich oppress you and drag you into the courts?" (James 2:5–6 NKJV). The situation that occasioned the instruction we find in these verses was undoubtedly an incident that James himself had witnessed. A group of people had assembled for public worship, and two strangers had come in. One was richly dressed, for his clothes are described as "fine apparel" (James 2:2 NKJV). On his finger was an ornate gold ring. Indeed, he seemed to be a man of wealth and social position. The second man was poorly dressed. Evidently he was a laboring man, for his clothes were worn and soiled. As they entered the Christian assembly, the rich man was ushered to the best seat and was told to sit "in a good place" (v. 3). The poor man was told to stand, or sit on the floor in some inconspicuous corner.

This, then, was the kind of situation that drew from James the words, "Have you not shown partiality among yourselves, and become judges with evil thoughts? Listen, my beloved brethren: Has God not chosen the poor of this world to be rich in faith and heirs of the kingdom which He promised to those who love Him? But you have dishonored the poor man. Do not the rich oppress you and drag you into the courts?" (James 2:4–6 NKJV). James makes it quite clear that this action violated a spiritual law. By their behavior the leaders of this church had implied that the soul of the rich man was more valuable than that of the poor man.

Needless to say, such an evaluation is not only totally false but an outrage on heaven itself. People whom God chooses are not those who are rich in wealth, but rather "rich in faith." It is both interesting and instructive to recall that historically speaking it is the poor, and not the rich, who generally respond to the call of the gospel (Luke 1:52; 1 Cor. 1:26–28). Ultimately, however, the kingdom of God is "promised to those who love Him" (James 2:5 NKJV).

But observe further that discrimination of persons is:

(2) The Violation of a Social Law

"But you have dishonored the poor man. Do not the rich oppress you and drag you into the courts? Do they not blaspheme that noble name by which you are called?" (James 2:6–7 NKJV). James shows that discrimination is unsociable if it makes dress, wealth, and power more important than souls, sinners, and saints. Indeed, in the original there is great indignation expressed in the words, "But you have dishonored the poor" (James 2:6 NKJV). The unreasonableness of such social discrimination is illustrated by the fact that so often it is the rich people who oppress the rest of society and draw men before the judgment seat and speak blasphemously of the worthy name of Jesus. As John Calvin comments, "It is an odd thing to honor one's executioners and in the meantime to injure one's friends." We cannot read through the Acts of the Apostles without seeing this principle demonstrated again and again (Acts 4:1–3; 13:50; 19:23–41); and church history confirms the same thing.

As we have seen already, God "has made from one blood every nation of men to dwell on all the face of the earth" (Acts 17:26 NKJV), and it is wholly unsociable and unconscionable to reject any member of the family of nations because of the lack of wealth, education, or influence. Such behavior demonstrates a failure to recognize the intrinsic worth of the human soul: "What will it profit a man if he gains the whole world, and loses his own soul?" (Mark 8:36 NKJV). Once again, discrimination is:

(3) The Violation of a Moral Law

"If you really fulfill the royal law according to the Scripture, 'You shall love your neighbor as yourself,' you do well; but if you show partiality, you commit sin, and are convicted by the law as transgressors. For whoever shall keep the whole law, and yet stumble in one point, he is guilty of all" (James 2:8–10 NKJV). James here quotes Leviticus 19:18 and describes God's law as "the royal law" because it is "the king of all laws," summing up man's relationship to man.

If anyone were to quibble as to who is a neighbor, the answer our Lord gave to a certain lawyer is absolutely clear. In his parable of the good Samaritan, he showed that there is no distinction (Luke 10:25–37); all men are neighbors, and we are to be concerned about our neighbors as we are concerned about ourselves. To act in this fashion is to "do well" (James 2:8 NKJV). On the other hand, to violate this royal law is to "commit sin" and to be "convicted by the law" (James 2:9 NKJV). Indeed, the author James goes on to liken this type of sin to adultery, murder, or the violation of any other aspect of the moral law.

Then to press home the seriousness of breaking God's law, he says, "For whoever shall keep the whole law, and yet stumble in one point, he is guilty of all" (James 2:10 NKJV). At first glance this may appear to be unfair and impracticable, but this is not so on closer examination.

D. L. Moody used to illustrate the reasonableness of God's demands by describing a man suspended over a cliff by a chain of ten links. "What happens," he would ask, "if all the links are broken? The answer, of course, is that the man falls to his doom." Then he would further press his point with this question: What happens if just one link is broken? The answer, of course, is the same—the man falls to his doom." Just as it takes one lie to make a liar, one theft to make a thief, one murder to make a murderer, so it takes just one act of discrimination to make a discriminator.

Some argue that those who belong to Christ are not under the law but under grace. The biblical answer to this piece of rationalization is that Jesus died and rose again to save us from the *curse* of the law, but not from the *claims* of the law (Rom. 8:3–4; 13:8–10). Christians should not be lawless; on the contrary, James implores: "So speak and so do as those who will be judged by the law of liberty. For judgment is without mercy to the one who has shown no mercy. Mercy triumphs over judgment" (James 2:12–13 NKJV).

So we see that "the answer to racial discrimination" is to keep the spiritual law, the social law, and the moral law. The spiritual law is based upon a common life shared in Jesus Christ by virtue of the new birth; the social law is based upon the intrinsic worth of man by reason of the fact that he is a member of the human family; the moral law is based upon God's command to love our neighbor as ourselves (Matt. 22:39).

One more consideration must engage our attention:

III. The Theological Answer to Racial Discrimination

"The Scripture says, 'Whoever believes on Him will not be put to shame.' For there is no distinction between Jew and Greek, for the same Lord over all is rich to all who call upon Him" (Rom. 10:11–12 NKJV). The body of divinity [theology] reveals without equivocation or even elucidation that God the Father loves all people, God the Son saves all people, and God the Holy Spirit claims all people without racial discrimination. With that as an opening preamble, let us proceed to examine each of the propositions a little more closely:

(1) God the Father Loves All People Without Discrimination

"For God so loved the world that He gave His only begotten Son, that whoever believes in Him should not perish but have everlasting life" (John 3:16 NKJV). When John gave expression to these words, he once and forever demolished the idea that God's love was discriminatory. This divine love includes *the world of mankind*. God acted in love to prove this. He came to this earth in the person of his Son and moved among men.

On three occasions the Gospel writers tell us that Jesus loved people. The first instance is that of the rich young ruler who came to him seeking to earn eternal life, and we are told that "Jesus, looking at him, loved him" (Mark 10:21 NKJV). Despite the fact that Christ's love was spurned, it is still true that Jesus loved him. Later on in the Savior's ministry we find him at the grave of Lazarus, where we see him weeping in sympathy with Mary and Martha because of the loss of their brother. The Jews who were looking on had to exclaim, "See how He loved him!" (John 11:36 NKJV). Then there is that great statement at the conclusion of his ministry, when we are told that "Jesus . . . having loved His own [disciples] who were in the world, He loved them to the end" (John 13:1 NKJV).

But more than this, Jesus demonstrated God's love for *the world of womankind*. All throughout human history the woman, for the most part, has been relegated to the place of inferiority and unimportance. This was never the purpose of God. From her very creation she has been regarded as of equal standing with man, and indeed, as his helpmate. Jesus came to restore this image both by his words and actions. It is written that "Jesus loved Martha and her sister" (John 11:5 NKJV). What Christianity has done to elevate womankind to a place that God has assigned for her is one of the splendid chapters of missionary endeavor.

But once again, Jesus came to demonstrate God's love for the *world of childkind*. Jesus could say, "Let the little children come to Me, and do not forbid them; for of such is the kingdom of God" (Mark 10:14 NKJV). These words were addressed to his beloved disciples when they attempted to shield the Master from the little ones who eagerly pressed toward him to receive his welcome and blessing. So it is that children throughout the world have been welcomed by the Savior, without respect for their class or color. Only the Christian gospel knows God as *Father*, and, therefore, as undiscriminating Love.

(2) God the Son Saves All People Without Discrimination

Christ "Himself is the propitiation for our sins, and not for ours only but also for *the whole world*" (1 John 2:2 NKJV, emphasis mine). The glory of the gospel is that Jesus Christ, God's Son, saves all people without discrimination. He saves people *wherever they are*. He told his disciples to "go into *all the world* and preach the gospel to *every creature*." And then he added, "He who believes and is baptized will be saved; but he who does not believe will be condemned" (Mark 16:15–16 NKJV, emphasis mine). Thank God, there are men, women, and children in every part of the world who have heard that gospel and have been saved and baptized.

God the Son saves people *whoever they are.* "There is no distinction between Jew and Greek, for the same Lord over all is rich to all who call upon Him. For 'whoever calls on the name of the Lord shall be saved'" (Rom. 10:12–13 NKJV). How wonderful to read those words—"The same Lord over all is rich to all who call upon Him"—

> "Red and yellow, black and white,
> All are precious in His sight."
> —Reverend C. H. Woolston

The only condition Jesus makes is that they must repent of their sins and call upon him in simple faith.

But once again, Jesus saves people *whatever they are.* Paul tells us in his first letter to the Corinthians that "not many wise according to the flesh, not many mighty, not many noble, are called" (1 Cor. 1:26 NKJV). You will notice that this verse does not say "not any" but rather "not many." This means that the basis of Christ's saving work is not conditioned by intellectual attainment, influential achievement, or even indigenous advancement, but simply on the grounds of the grace of God and the response of man.

Yes, God the Son saves all people without racial discrimination. With God the Father and God the Son:

(3) God the Spirit Claims All People Without Discrimination

On the day of Pentecost Peter told his audience that the Holy Spirit was poured out upon "all flesh" (Acts 2:17 NKJV), and subsequent events reveal this to be true.

God the Spirit claimed the Jews. The greatest example of the regenerating power of the Spirit among Jews was the conversion of Saul of Tarsus, recorded for us in Acts 9. If ever there were a bigoted intellectual, it was this young Jewish zealot who hated the name of Jesus and harassed the church of God in every city.

Then came that moment in history when the Spirit of God laid claim to Saul of Tarsus. In a flash of blinding light he was translated from the kingdom of darkness into the kingdom of light, from the service of Satan to the service of Jesus Christ.

Of all people in New Testament times, Paul was one of the greatest witnesses to the saving grace of God. In his own words he tells us: "I thank Christ Jesus our Lord who has enabled me, because He counted me faithful, putting me into the ministry, although I was formerly a blasphemer, a persecutor, and an insolent man; but I obtained mercy because I did it ignorantly in unbelief. And the grace of our Lord was exceedingly abundant, with faith and love which are in Christ Jesus. This is a faithful saying and worthy of all acceptance, that Christ Jesus came into the world to save sinners, of whom I am chief. However, for this reason I obtained mercy, that in me first Jesus Christ might show all longsuffering, as a pattern to those who are going to believe on Him for everlasting life" (1 Tim. 1:12–16 NKJV).

God the Spirit claimed the Greeks. In Acts 16 we read of the occasion when Paul came to Derbe and Lystra and "behold, a certain disciple was there, named Timothy, the son of a certain Jewish woman who believed, but his father was *Greek*" (v. 1 NKJV). That boy responded to the message of the gospel and became Paul's son in the faith and, in many senses, his successor in the ministry. Here, then, was a Greek who was claimed by God the Holy Spirit. Dr. Luke was also a Greek. He was a native of Antioch, a physician, and a faithful companion and assistant to the apostle Paul. Like Timothy, he was also claimed by God the Holy Spirit.

God the Spirit claimed the Romans. Among the stories we could cite is the example of Cornelius of Caesarea, a centurion of the band called the Italian Band. We read that he was a devout man, one who feared God with all his house, and a man who gave much alms to the people and prayed always; and yet he was unregenerate (Acts 10:1–48). God had to rid Peter of racial prejudice in order that he might send him to the house of Cornelius to lead this centurion to a saving knowledge of Christ. And we read that "Peter opened his mouth and said: 'In truth I perceive that *God shows no partiality*'" (Acts 10:34 NKJV, emphasis mine), and as he preached Christ, the Holy Spirit fell on all them who heard the word, and a notable Roman was gloriously saved.

God the Spirit claimed the Ethiopians. This story is told graphically and dramatically in Acts 8:26–40. The man in question was known as a eunuch of great authority under Candace, queen of the Ethiopians. As chancellor of the exchequer, he had charge of all her treasure and was a man of obvious brilliance and intelligence. Dissatisfied in his soul, he came to Jerusalem to worship and find solace; but disillusioned and disappointed, he started on his way home. Dr. Luke records how God chose his servant, Philip, the evangelist, and compelled him by the urging of the Spirit to leave a revival in Samaria to seek out this lonely Ethiopian in the desert of Gaza. The encounter led to his conversion. Claimed by the Spirit and baptized into Christ, the Ethiopian went on his way rejoicing—and taking with him a transforming gospel for his fellow Ethiopians in North Africa.

If you have followed this illustrative treatment of our subject, you have observed that no one can accept the Bible as the Word of God and be a respecter of persons. Clearly, racial discrimination is sociologically untenable, nomologically unethical, and theologically unbiblical. Let us then demonstrate true Christian discipleship by having love one for another (John 13:35). And in demonstrating such love, remember Christ's high priestly prayer as he anticipated his reconciling death on the cross of Calvary: Father, he cried, "as We are one . . . may [they, and those of us living today] be made perfect in one, and that the world may know that You have sent Me, and have loved them as You have loved Me" (John 17:22–23 NKJV).

How awesome it is to realize that the answer to *that prayer,* humanly speaking, depends on you and me! Let us ponder solemnly these words before we sing again:

> We are one in the Spirit, we are one in the Lord,
> We are one in the Spirit, we are one in the Lord,
> And we pray that all unity may one day be restored:
> And they'll know we are Christians by our love,
>   by our love,
> Yes, they'll know we are Christians by our love.

—Peter Scholtes[2]

Chapter 5

Love: Fundamental Ingredient of the Christian Life

MICHAEL F. THURMAN
1 John 3:11–18

In this passage of Scripture, John the elder becomes most practical in his thinking. His advice to the church is now presented at grass-roots level. There are no thrills and shrills in this bit of advice to the church; just plain, ordinary, fundamental instructions: "Love is synonymous with life, and death is synonymous with hate." He demonstrates love as opposed to hate by a vivid and well-known biblical illustration of the evil act of Cain murdering his brother Abel. For John, the Christian life is a life enveloped with the characteristic of love, as both inward and outward manifestations of personal commitments to Jesus Christ. "We know," John says, "that we have passed from death to

MICHAEL F. THURMAN is pastor of Dexter Avenue King Memorial Baptist Church in Montgomery, Alabama. He is a graduate of Morehouse College (B.A.) and New Orleans Baptist Theological Seminary (M.Div.). Prior to accepting his present pastoral charge, Reverend Thurman served as associate director of the Black Church Extension Division of the North American Mission Board of the Southern Baptist Convention. A popular preacher and conference leader, he has spoken in numerous church and seminary settings on evangelism, church planting, and discipleship. He is a member of the Association of Black Sociologists and is currently engaged in research on the Revitalization of Historical African-American Churches sponsored by the Louisville Institute, a program of the Lilly Endowment.. This sermon was originally presented from the same pulpit from which Dr. Martin Luther King Jr. preached during his historic ministry in Montgomery.

life, because we love the brethren" (1 John 3:14 NKJV). For John this was the social test that was to reveal true Christian identity. He also included a moral and a doctrinal test.

As we explore the church of our day, there is little doubt that the nineteen-hundred-year-old message continues to be relevant. If John were invited to speak to the churches of our times, a message on the importance of love would be quite appropriate. Loves seems to be the forgotten element in many churches.

The need for love, both to love others and to be loved by others, is a basic human need. C. S. Lewis in his book *The Weight of Glory; and Other Addresse*s states that "the ultimate preference of the will for love rather than hatred, and happiness rather than misery comprise basic moral intuitions of consciousness which cannot be disputed. These are the very voice of humanity."

Let us explore this element of love as it finds expression in the life of the church.

I. Upon the mandate to "love one another" rests the fundamental principle for living the Christian life.

It is quite explicit that the act of loving one another is of supreme importance to the Christian faith. In essence, to love others is the Christian thing to do. Apart from our love for God, love for our fellowman is foundational in living the Christian life. When Christ was approached by the Pharisees and the Sadducees, and one of them asked, "Master, which is the great commandment in the law?"(Matt. 22:36), his reply was "Thou shalt love the Lord thy God with all thy heart, and with all thy soul, and with all thy mind. This is the first and great commandment. And the second is like unto it, Thou shalt love thy neighbour as thyself. On these two commandments hang all the law and the prophets" (Matt. 22:37–40).

From this passage we see the cross of Jesus to be two-dimensional. The vertical beam reaches upward from earth to heaven, symbolizing man's desperate attempt to formulate a relationship with God. The horizontal beam reaches outward, symbolizing man as he desperately tries to formulate and maintain meaningful relationships with other members of human society. Our responsibilities do not reach an abrupt end when we enter into a personal relationship with God through Christ, but by the very nature of that unique relationship we are called upon to enter into relationships with fellow human beings.

To love others is easier said than done; however, we must manage to incorporate it into our daily lives. We must wrestle with, and ultimately overcome, our prejudices that we bring to bear on the relationships we form with others. Our love for others must be based on our recognition of them as having desires and needs just as we do, as having the basic sameness as we, as having a truly transcendent reality about themselves as we do. Again, C. S. Lewis states: "There are no ordinary people. You have never talked to a mere mortal. Nations, cultures, arts, civilizations—these are mortal, and their life to ours as the life of a gnat. But it is immortals whom we joke with, work with, marry, snub, and exploit—immortal horrors or everlasting splendors."

As Augustine, the great pillar of the Christian church, once said, "Envy is incompatible with love . . . there can be no envy in love." There is no room for the two traits to occupy the same vessel, for one is diametrically opposed to the other. Somehow we must come to grips with Thomas Jefferson's statement that "all men are created equal."

Isn't it amazing how when we enter into relationships we bring with us our own prejudices? We assess our dealings with others based on our personal, and often very subjective, likes and dislikes. "I don't want to be associated with him because he is loud." "I am cautious how I deal with him or her because he or she does not belong to the same socioeconomic class as I." "I don't really like the way he or she dresses; therefore, I will maintain a distance from him or her, so as not to ruin my reputation."

These prejudices are often the nurturing ground from which full-blown hatred develops. Hatred is contrary to God's way. We must somehow learn to give each other mutual respect, and recognize that all human lives have value. When we discriminate against others, we are in essence playing God, for God alone is allowed to be discriminating. Note that God is not a discriminating God, for he allows his sun to "rise on the evil and on the good" (Matt. 5:45).

"The concept of reverence for personality then is applicable between persons from whom, in the initial instance, the heavy weight of status has been sloughed off. Then what? Each person meets the other where he is and treats him as if he were where he ought to be."[1]

Perhaps there is no single reason that addresses the fact that "love is the fundamental ingredient of the Christian life" better than God's way is the way of love and not hate.

Paul Hoon states that "love is a requirement which the universe itself imposes upon man. Ethical love is not an option, nor an invention of priest or moralist, nor an evolutionary sport. Love confronts men as a Christian categorical imperative from the heart of Reality . . . . Christian love, while embodied in the church, is applicable to all human relations and can meet the demands of every individual and social situation without losing its dignity, power, and eternity."[2]

Let us remember that we have been issued a mandate by John the elder: we absolutely must love one another. Love can overcome the differences we share and can form a bond that cannot be broken between the most opposite of human spirits. "Love conquers all," it has been said. That is exactly what the world needs to see. It needs to see that Christian love cannot only strive inside the institutional church but also that it is capable of bending down in physical form and ministering patiently to the most horrible of human conditions that exist outside the church. In order to be an effective witness for Christ, Christian love must get outside the comfort of the four walls and move freely among a hurting society.

The church needs to minister to those who smell of alcohol, to those who show deterioration from the use of drugs, and to those who are victims of poverty. The church has a responsibility to young teenage girls who become pregnant, to offer a helping hand in child care in order that they may be able to stay in school and excel despite their mistakes. The church has a mandate to provide ministries for the elderly and to involve the elderly in ministries in order that they can experience a heightened sense of self-worth in their golden years. God sides with love, "for God is love," as John the elder affirms in 1 John 4:8 (NKJV).

To be like God is to live a life filled with love. Love must become an integral part of our being.

II. We can theorize about the Christian life being comprised of love all we want, but the mandate guards against mere lip service and moves us to action.

John gets quite specific at this point. The message is conveyed in simple and clear language. "Because He [Christ] laid down His life for us. And we also ought to lay down our lives for the brethren" (1 John 3:16 NKJV). John is speaking of sacrificial love. He goes on in verse 18 to say, "let us not love in word, neither in tongue [speech NRSV]; but in deed and in truth."

Even James in his letter to the church jumps on this bandwagon in chapter 2:15–16: "If a brother or sister be naked, and destitute of daily food, and one of you [the church] say unto them, Depart in peace, be ye warmed and filled; notwithstanding ye give them not those things which are needful to the body; what doth it profit?" John says that this kind of action, or rather the lack of action, is ungodly. "How can the love of God dwell in him?" (1 John 3:17).

New Testament Christianity guards against the idea of social indifference, and it places demands upon the church to be a dynamic organism that is built upon a holistic view of man. A church that ministers only to the spiritual needs of its constituents and fails to minister to the physical needs has not taken seriously the mandate of Christ. It is not an either-or approach, but it is a both-and approach. True love for God is not expressed in sentimental languages or mystical experience, but in moral obedience. Furthermore, no religious experience is valid if it does not have moral consequences.

The idea here is that those who have been the recipients of God's love are most likely to be the ones who because of their experiences of love will be willing to share it with others. Only those who have been the object of love can in turn focus that love on others.

It is beyond the wildest imagination as to how the most opposite of people can be bound by the common denominator of love. It is under the auspices of love that human spirits from different polarities become knit together in an effort to aid people in despair.

Some years ago as a child I can remember attending several churches in the Montgomery area. I began to notice there was a blind man and two little boys who would come to those churches seeking assistance. The man seemed to have been inflicted with glandular problems as well as a limp that accompanied his every step. The clothes he wore were often dirty and ragged, but I never saw that man denied. The churches, even the smallest ones, would contribute something to his well-being. Their spirits were woven together in Christian love as they shared of their resources with this man. They did not pat him on the back and say, "My prayers are with you." They ministered to his needs.

That is what John refers to in 1 John 3:17–18: "If any one has the world's goods and sees his brother in need, yet closes his heart against him, how does God's love abide in him? Little children, let us not love in word or speech but in deed and in truth" (RSV). The church is the visible community of God's people who express his love toward others.

This is a fundamental step in learning to live like Christ. Christ gave to us his life because he loved us; therefore, we must be willing to sacrifice our lives for others.

III. Love will never reach its fullest expression in the realm of the flesh; it reaches its ultimate fulfillment on a higher plane.

Within this world the greatest hindrance to our acting within the boundaries of love is the viciousness of human greed. Human greed and agape love cannot share in the same experience; the two are contradictory. Whenever the two attempt to operate together, greed usually overshadows agape love temporarily. For it presents its trappings that few can resist.

Whenever the city of man governs society, there is corruption, crime, vice, racism, and injustice. This is because human nature is basically evil. The quest for power, control, money, and the tenets of greed are rampant within the city of man. As long as we live in the city of man, we will be faced with the powerful vices of racism, nationalism, sexism, creedalism, classism, and all of the other "isms" that keep us divided.

The city of God on earth depends upon born-again men and women and children; renewed persons whose hearts have been changed; the new Jerusalem, the church, people who know the laws that govern kingdom living.

It starts in the heart of one person and moves to the heart of another. It happens individually and then moves among family groups, and then it impacts neighborhoods, institutions, cities, states, regions, nations, and finally the world.

Let us close by looking at perhaps the greatest treatise ever written on love. That is none other than the thirteenth chapter of 1 Corinthians written by the apostle Paul.

If I speak in the tongues of men and of angels, but have not love, I am only a resounding gong or a clanging cymbal. If I have the gift of prophecy and can fathom all mysteries and all knowledge, and if I have a faith that can move mountains, but have not love, I am nothing. If I give all I possess to the poor and surrender my body to the flames, but have not love, I gain nothing. Love is patient, love is kind. It does not envy, it does not boast, it is not proud. It is not rude, it is not self-seeking, it is not easily angered, it keeps no record of wrongs. Love does not delight in evil but rejoices with the truth. It always protects, always trusts, always hopes, always perseveres. Love never fails. But where there are prophecies, they will cease; where there are tongues, they will be stilled; where there is knowledge, it will pass away. For we know in part and we prophesy in part, but when perfection comes, the imperfect disappears. When I was a child, I talked like a child, I thought like a child, I reasoned like a child. When I became a man, I put childish ways behind me. Now we see but a poor reflection as in a mirror; then we shall see face to face. Now I know in part; then I shall know fully, even as I am fully known. And now these three remain: faith, hope and love. But the greatest of these is love. (NIV)

Chapter 6

Destination Inclusion

JAY WOLF

Acts 10

"Remember the Alamo!" was our taunting cry.

Those words inspired the Texas Freedom Fighters in 1836, but in 1963 I used that hallowed battle cry as a result of the infection of prejudice. My target was the Spanish-flavored kids who committed the crime of being different from me.

After our third-grade day was over in Georgetown, Texas, a gang of us white kids would square off against the Mexican boys. I still have vivid memories of those "Remember the Alamo" rock fights. In addition to the stones we hurled, we gathered all the nasty names we had learned and lobbed those verbal grenades at our dark-skinned adversaries. At the tender age of nine, I was already initiated into the sick game of discrimination and exclusion.

JAY WOLF *is pastor of First Baptist Church, Montgomery, Alabama, a position he has held since 1991. A native of Georgetown, Texas, Wolf studied at Baylor University (B.A.) and New Orleans Baptist Theological Seminary (M.Div.). From 1984 until 1991, he was pastor of First Baptist Church, Alexandria, Virginia, during which time he also served as honorary chaplain for the United States Senate. He is a member of the Evangelism Strategy Task Force of the Baptist World Alliance, and the Executive Committee of the Alabama Baptist State Board of Missions. In this sermon, "Destination Inclusion," he recounts something of his own personal journey from racial prejudice toward the gospel of acceptance. He also provides practical suggestions for applying this liberating message both in personal living and congregational action.*

My Path

In the 1960s, I was trying to grow up in central Texas as the nation was trying to grow up and become mature enough to birth authentic civil rights for all its citizens. A fellow Texan and White House occupant, Lyndon B. Johnson, was developing "the Great Society," which advocated the dignity and practical equality of all of his fellow Americans. Transformative legislation was eliminating the absurdly demeaning tools of segregation that included separate water fountains, divided public seating, and education discrimination. Courageous jurists like Judge Frank Johnson, of Montgomery, Alabama, led the charge that forced our society to examine its nonsensical practice of prejudice.

My life transformation was not linked to national legislation or the judiciary but rather to a personal encounter with Jesus Christ that rerouted my eternal destiny and core values. Dad— Jay Wolf Sr.—was a Texas rancher and aggressive entrepreneur. Five Wolf cubs inhabited our family. My parents were good people, but they shared the prejudices of their era. Black and Hispanic Americans were generally referred to in derogatory terms, not as a matter of hatred, but as a reflection of playing the culturally created game of exclusion.

As the Wizard of Oz said to the brain-desiring Scarecrow, "You are a victim of confused thinking!" "Confused thinking" regarding other races seemed to reign within our American society, our home, and within my personal view of God's human creation. Like the vast majority of the planet, I needed to feel superior to someone else. Out of our need for superiority, we build relational fences to keep dissimilar people out instead of bridges to let all people in. My conjecture is that the need for superiority drives the spread of the virulent plague of prejudice, discrimination, and exclusivism.

As I look back on my early years with a clearer vision, the soil of ignorance, selfishness, and inherent sinfulness grew an abundant crop of the noxious weeds of personal prejudice. Consequently, the Hispanic and black children in my elementary school were viewed as inferior. When you lost something due to childish incompetence, you naturally assumed one of the dark-skinned children took it. Our playground reflected the sickness of society through the "Remember the Alamo" rock fights and the perpetual cliquishness of children. The birds of our feather flew tightly together and did not graft "ugly ducklings" into the flock. I was definitely an excluder and not an includer.

A pivotal life experience occurred for me when a relative died in Johnson City, Texas. After attending the funeral, my young mind began to calculate the realities of death. I became extremely frightened when I used my relative's earthly departure as a mirror to examine the features of my own mortality. This event, coupled with the coaching of me by a sincere Christian children's worker at the First Baptist Church of Georgetown, led me to a path of personally exploring God's Word.

As a twelve-year-old, I developed a new daily discipline of reading the Bible. My Dad, who was my hero and pal, expressed astonishment at my growing religious interest. I was like a hungry kid in a free candy store. I devoured the Word of God and its transforming truth. The light of Christ began to illuminate my heart. I personalized God's core truth that Jesus loved me and gave his life for me. I was captivated by the amazing truth that Jesus included even me! My growing faith motivated me to trust Christ to forgive the sinful attitudes of self-sufficiency that separated me from God and seek adoption into his forever family. When I caught the infection of Christianity, I received a full-blown case of the real disease!

After Jesus saved my soul, his indwelling Spirit began the process of metamorphosizing a culturally bound caterpillar into a flight-ready butterfly. As one earthy theologian put it, "Jesus gets a man out of hell in a second, but it takes a lifetime to get the hell out of a man." In more specific terms, I asked God to take this little lump of clay named *Jay* and mold me into the image of Jesus each day. After affecting my eternal destination, Christ put me on the path of transforming my temporal value system.

The steady flow of God's Word into my spiritual engine pushed me forward in my faith journey and gave me the moral energy to climb some big hills. By the time I was sixteen years old, I clearly sensed God's direction to use the stewardship of my gifts to become a builder of God's kingdom. Dad wanted me to be a lawyer. My dream was to make bales of money, own a big chunk of the material world, and exert influence over others. Yet, God steered my little boat away from the magnetism of materialism as he torqued my core values 180 degrees in the opposite direction.

Like leaven-permeating dough, God's truth was infiltrating every crevice of my thinking. Jesus was deeply impacting my vocabulary, vocational direction, and core values. On the spiritual level, I felt equivalent to a young athlete who is being transformed through an aggressive weight-training program. The workouts were yielding the fruit of authentic change.

For instance, my view of people was now passing through the filters of God's love. It dawned on me that all people mattered to God. After all, Jesus died for everyone. I reasoned from Genesis and the creation account that all people were made in God's image and consequently worthy of dignity and respect regardless of their age, size of their wages, or color of their skin. Additionally, the sledgehammer-like truth of 1 John 4 crashed into the fences of exclusion that I had constructed. With piercing logic, God's Word clearly instructed that it is impossible to say you love God whom you have not seen and simultaneously hate your neighbor whom you have seen. I was checkmated!

As God was orchestrating a shifting of my internal value system, these changes converged with an opportunity to start a Young Life club at Georgetown High School. Understanding that God cared for all people and he wanted to cast an outreach net within our school that would provide a clear witness for Christ, I decided to join the Father in that fabulous adventure of being on his redeem team. I instigated the formation of a Young Life club as a voice for Christ and a tool for evangelism on our campus.

In order to strategize the club's formation, we had an organizational meeting at my home. Our ranch was west of Georgetown and was bordered by Highway 29 and the San Gabriel River. Our version of a Wolf den was a large two-story colonial home perched above the picturesque river and surrounded by hundreds of acres of live oak-decorated central Texas hill country. For our important strategy meeting, I invited a Hispanic student and a black friend who were my brothers in Christ and buddies who played on the basketball team.

When our strategy session was concluded and everyone had left, my mother told me that it was inappropriate to have a black and a Hispanic student in our home because they were good candidates to come back later and burglarize the place. I protested Mother's tainted concern by pointing out that my friends' faith made them eternal relatives and unlikely to become future felons.

Mom was a good person, but she carried a big dose of the disease of her day—the plague of prejudice. We had an open discussion about God's instructions to see all people through his eyes of love and acceptance. The discussion was as productive as watering plastic flowers. But for the first time, I was forced to articulate how Jesus had called me beyond my "Remember the Alamo" rock-fighting prejudices into a new view of all people based on his view instead of my natural bent to be exclusionary. I realized that Jesus had touched my eyes and was in the process of making me color-blind. He was moving me along the path of becoming an includer.

God's revelation of inclusion grew clearer when I discovered the truth of Acts 10. In that amazing encounter, the Father scheduled a barrier-breaking meeting that included Peter, Cornelius, and his culture-cracking Holy Spirit. The God who made the blind to see was about to make the seeing color-blind.

The Biblical Map for Inclusion: Peter's Path

If you travel from New Orleans up the Mississippi River 2,348 miles, you will be at Lake Itaska, Minnesota, the headwaters of America's most famous waterway. Similarly, Acts 10 represents the headwaters of the Gentile church. Our inclusive heavenly Father cares for all people, and his servant Peter was in dire need of learning that lesson. Acts 10 finds God in the process of routing his special spokesman upstream to the refreshing waters of inclusion.

Like my parents and my family, Peter was a product of his era. The Jews tended to classify their world into two parts: the chosen people of God—Israel—and everybody else, the Gentiles. Peter had witnessed firsthand the inclusion of Jesus. Peter witnessed Christ shattering every Jewish prejudice when the Master included the multimarried Samaritan women. The big fisherman must have watched with a slacked jaw as Jesus embraced every type of social reject. Peter heard with his own ears the discrimination-exploding tale of the "good Samaritan." While Peter had observed the lessons of inclusion, he had not yet come to the point of applying them. Like the vast majority of those who claim followship of Jesus, Peter was educated beyond his obedience!

The good news of God's love and forgiveness was designed for the whole planet, yet the gospel's dissemination was being restricted by prejudice. The overall theme of the Book of Acts is the shattering of barriers by the sledgehammer of the gospel. The dynamite of the gospel had exploded the barriers of Judaism, materialism, paganism, geography, and now the next tough target would be prejudice.

As we join Peter's journey, we find him in the seaside village of Joppa. Prior to his arrival, he experienced the explosive gospel breaking through the barrier of death. A wonderful follower of Jesus named Dorcas had expired, and Peter was inspired to intercede on her behalf. As a result of this dramatic faith exercise, Dorcas did an imitation of Jesus by resurrecting. God was glorified and a barrier-breaking witness was shared. After doing the difficult work of resuscitating the dead, Peter needed a break.

Peter had a pal at Joppa named Simon the Tanner. While the lodging at Simon's house was free, there was a surcharge that came in the form of odor. If you have ever smelled a tannery, there is no mystery about Peter spending time on the roof! In addition to seeking fresher fragrances, the ocean air would be invigorating. Join Peter through the theater of your imagination and you can feel the refreshing Mediterranean breeze waft over your body. Listen, and you can hear the rhythm of the surf gently calling you to tranquillity.

Peter records in his chronology that around noontime, while in the middle of a soothing season of prayer, perhaps with a growling stomach, he fell into a trance. During these mystical moments reality was suspended, and God sent a vision from his heart to the head of this strategic servant. An enormous sheet descended from heaven. The sheet became a tablecloth containing all kinds of animals and crawling creatures. A heavenly invitation came to the famished fisherman instructing Peter to arise, kill, and eat. Peter protested by retreating into the kosher dietary restrictions of his Jewish heritage. Twice more, the heavenly voice urged Peter to eat and understand that everything God had created was inherently clean.

Suddenly, the vision evaporated and Peter stepped back from his trance into the reality of his rooftop perch above the tannery. With the vivid vision lingering on his mind, Peter quickly calculated the true meaning of this far-reaching revelation. He deduced that the vision was not about pigs but about people. Through this eureka experience of illumination, Peter comprehended that God's rules about what is clean and unclean had been misinterpreted. He clearly understood that the restrictions separating Jews and Gentiles were about to be abolished. The gospel sledgehammer was cocked and ready to splinter another barrier!

For generations, the Jews had carefully compartmentalized animals and people into the categories of clean and unclean. The Jewish interpretation of the Levitical law had become warped into a tight and ugly exclusivism. The halo of desired purity had become a strangling noose of exclusivity. Instead of becoming the fulfillment of the Abrahamic Covenant that instructed the Jewish nation to be a blessing to all nations, the chosen people of God became a closed clique. Judaism was not the refreshing, redemptive river of God's blessing but more closely resembled the nonproductive Dead Sea. The blessings of God had been twisted into pride, prejudice, superiority, and bigotry. The halo had become a noose, and the purposes of God were being strangled.

The Jewish nation had taken the boards of God's blessing and built a fence around themselves instead of a bridge to persons of other cultures who were in desperate need of meeting their Creator. The Lord was about to take the gospel worldwide. A prejudiced Jewish fisherman on the rooftop of a small tannery was soon to become God's tool for demolishing the barrier of discrimination.

Peter the Redneck

Why did God pick Peter for this task? In my estimate, he was the perfect candidate for dismantling the Jewish fence of bigotry. Peter was the first-century prototype for a racist redneck. A little-known scholarly hypothesis indicates that Peter's middle name may have been "Bubba!" If camels could have been equipped with gun racks and heavy mud-grip tires, that would have been Peter's model. Peter was a Galilean version of Archie Bunker. No doubt this blustery, outspoken, blue-collared laborer participated in his own version of a "Remember the Alamo" rock fight. Yet, the transformative power of Jesus Christ was about to reach into another crevice of Peter's heart and bring cleansing. The Lord Jesus was going to make Peter his "poster child" to demonstrate that even the stubborn stronghold of racism can be bulldozed by God's love.

How are you doing in the area of discrimination? No, I'm not referring to your sanitized theories and politically correct responses on racism. How are you really doing in the Christ-flavored lifestyle of becoming an includer? Perhaps you skipped "Remember the Alamo" rock fight episodes. Or perhaps your categorization of people is not so much by color but instead by status. Discrimination can come dressed in many ugly costumes.

Perhaps your exclusion is based on economics or the lack thereof. Do you instantly grade a person as inferior or superior to yourself when you find out his or her educational level? Some people go through life with their noses stuck high into the air because their physique and physical conditioning is a notch superior to Mr. and Mrs. Average. Your financial condition, educational achievements, social position, physical fitness, job title, and neighborhood address can all be fuel for feeding the infection of exclusivism. If someone is significantly different, we tend to reflexively reject.

Yet, in rejecting another person, we essentially reject the core of the gospel. My model for inclusion is Jesus. The apostle Paul would reason from Christ's example in Romans 15:7 that we should "accept one another, just as Christ also accepted us" (NASB).

We learned earlier in Acts 10 that God had been at work in the life of a man named Cornelius. On another channel, God transmitted a vision to this spiritually sensitive Roman soldier. In a transmission of divine affirmation, the Lord let Cornelius know that he was connecting to the true emperor of the universe. God's radar screen registered this Roman. For the rest of the story, Cornelius needed to dispatch some couriers to Joppa to receive the unabridged version from Peter. By the orchestration of God, Peter's prejudice-shattering vision converged with Cornelius's invitation. Like mixing gas and fire, the Gentile explosion was about to occur.

The Gospel Unbound

Without hesitation, Peter responded to the stranger's invitation to meet this Roman God-seeker. Peter's mind must have been flooded with questions. After all, it wasn't long ago that a Roman centurion had directed the murder of Jesus, and it would be a Roman cross that would eventually hold Peter's body. Was this a ploy? Should he be afraid? To his credit, Peter subordinated his fears to his faith and journeyed with his guides toward the destination of inclusion.

Upon arriving at Cornelius's home, introductions and explanations were exchanged. After Cornelius shared a summary of his vision, Peter sounded his primary good-news note. Similar to his undiluted message of Pentecost, Peter succinctly explained that Jesus is the Messiah of God and the Savior of all who will trust him. Peter explained the crucifixion and resurrection of Jesus. The fisher of souls completed his message by identifying himself as a messenger of God's Good News of forgiveness. Before the invitational net could be drawn and the sinner's prayer offered, there was a Holy Spirit explosion!

Suddenly, a host of these unkosher, noncircumcised Gentile believers were speaking in an unknown tongue and praising God. This was an exterior confirmation of an interior transformation! The barrier was demolished. Peter was completely convinced of the authenticity of their conversion.

Peter instructed these newly included members of Christ's family to further symbolize their new life in the Lord by experiencing a believer's baptism. Peter spent a few extra days in the discipling process. He probably sampled pork chops too!

Peter returned to headquarters in Jerusalem armed with God's clear revelation of inclusion, which was vividly demonstrated by Cornelius's conversion. Peter unflinchingly proclaimed that the gospel is for everyone. The barrier of racism was broken. Furthermore, the Lord expects his followers to continue dismantling the walls that divide us and construct relational bridges to all people at all times.

APPLICATION: *Strategies for Arriving at Destination Inclusion*

1. Follow Peter's path and refuse to substitute your bias, comfort, or culture for the clear instruction of the Lord. Give heart-attack-like seriousness to God's truth. Ananias and Sapphira wish they had! God's character and Word mandate the repudiation of discrimination and the implementation of inclusion. Authentic Christians must be includers. Can I communicate it any more clearly than that?

2. Then move from theological contemplation to obedient Christ-honoring action. The following initiatives comprise additional strategies:

Extend simple acts of courtesy and kindness to people you encounter daily who are different from you. This obvious truth was graphically underlined for me by my friend, Steve Roberts. Steve teaches at a predominately black high school in Montgomery, Alabama. One day we were visiting the hospital together, and he observed that I passed several black people in the hospital corridor and did not acknowledge them. Steve suggested a better way. "When you see a stranger, especially a dark-skinned person, you can be a great encourager for Christ and racial reconciliation if you will take the time to make eye contact and offer a sincere greeting." Develop the reflex of inclusion by communicating kindness and respect as you encounter people in the daily traffic patterns.

Willard Scott, the famous TV personality, made a similar observation a few years ago. Willard grew up attending the First Baptist Church of Alexandria, Virginia. When I was pastor of that congregation in 1987, I invited Willard to speak for a Sunday morning service. He shared an intriguing story of inclusion linked to small kindnesses.

He told us about playing the role of McDonald's first official "Ronald McDonald" in the late 1960s. At a public appearance as the chain's mascot in Washington, D.C., he noticed a black child and her dad standing near him. The child's shoe was untied. Willard was in his Ronald outfit, but he reflexively stooped and tied the girl's shoe and gave her a big hug.

Several years later, Willard met the child's father. This black gentleman explained that he was a very prejudiced man who hated white people. But when Scott tied his child's shoe, something inside his bigoted heart became untied. He went on to share with Willard that a simple act of color-blind inclusion began to melt a heart that had been frozen by discrimination. Willard Scott encouraged us to use the little opportunities of daily living to touch people with God's inclusive love.

Get acquainted with someone who is different from you. Perhaps the difference is skin color, age, economic status, lifestyle viewpoint, or cultural orientation. Ignorance breeds fear and knowledge births understanding. I had a friend who was afraid of heights, so he took a course on sky diving! The same Christian friend feared small children, so he became a nursery worker at our church! Motivated by Christ's admonition to be a victor and not a victim, he faced his fears and squashed them. Face the fears generated by dissimilarities so you can connect and conquer.

Construct some bonding activities. Participating in team sports has the unusual power of creating cohesion. I am incredibly close to some friends who play racquetball and tennis with me. Explore and determine a mutual interest and go do it. Sharing a game of tennis, a fishing excursion, or a sporting event could construct a lifetime friendship. If something as monumental as a lifetime friendship does not occur, at least newfound knowledge can erase fears and replace bigotry with appreciation.

Worship together. There is an old saying, "The ground is level at the foot of the cross." When we engage in worship, we are momentarily measuring our lives against the backdrop of eternity. Authentic worship allows us to clear away the daily debris and see the face of God. Simultaneously, we are enabled to calculate what is truly important and of lasting significance. The debris-like differences that divide us can float away through a worship experience and be replaced by a bond that is stronger than Super Glue. In my own experience, a dear African-American brother named Leon Baker has accompanied our First Baptist team to four "Promise Keepers" events. As I worshiped beside Leon, the white heat of God's purifying presence fused our souls. I count Leon in a special, intense circle of my closest of kin because worship has welded us together as brothers in Christ.

Lift a load together. Intentionally identify someone who is different from you and invite him or her to do a task. For example, at First Baptist we have a tutoring program. We invite children from the impoverished neighborhood of Tulane Court to come to First Baptist during the school year and receive supper, a witness for Christ, and individual instruction linked to their school work. This experience of lifting a load together, the load of learning, has broken down the wall of discrimination and built the bridge of inclusion in the hearts of the students and tutors.

Another example is a Habitat for Humanity project. Our First Baptist crew shared the building of a Habitat house with our partner church, Hutchinson Missionary Baptist Church, whose membership is predominately black. Additionally, our two churches hosted Florida State coach Bobby Bowden for a special service focused on racial reconciliation. Doing these projects together created a unique sense of teamwork that comes from lifting a common load. We not only built a Habitat for Humanity structure for a family and provided a powerful service for the city with Coach Bowden, but lasting friendships were built as dividing walls of prejudice were destroyed.

Live out God's instruction to "accept one another as Christ has accepted you," and you will soon arrive at Destination Inclusion!

Chapter 7

"Who Is My Neighbor?"

GERALD AUSTIN SR.

Luke 10:25–37

A neighbor is someone who lives close by. When we apply this in a literal sense to our individual situations, we can easily conclude that those people who are close to us are our neighbors. In a sense, we could even conclude that neighbors are those people similar to us.

The question of "Who is my neighbor?" never really occurred to me until early 1980. I had just read a brilliant article written by a group of sociologists, anthropologists, and economists. The title of the article was "The Bifurcation of the Classes." This distinguished group of well-educated social scientists concluded from their research that the chasm between the middle and lower

GERALD AUSTIN SR. *is the founder and president of the Center for Urban Missions and also pastor of The New City Church in Birmingham, Alabama. Reverend Austin is one of nine children raised by a single parent in the housing projects of the community where he now ministers. After academic training and a successful career in electronic engineering, Austin responded to God's call to serve the church in the inner city. He has been coordinator of black church development for Missions to North America, an outreach ministry of the Presbyterian Church in America. His theological training includes graduate studies at the Center for Urban Theological Studies in Philadelphia and at Beeson Divinity School of Samford University.*

Austin is highly respected as a community activist and innovative leader in multicultural ministries in the Birmingham area. He and his wife, Gwen, who is a partner with her husband in ministry, are the parents of six children.

class was widening. As a result there is little hope for those in our lower-class, poor and hurting communities. This was a very strong indictment coming from such noted authorities. Many people of our day and time have bought into this sense of hopelessness, even as I had.

I am one of nine children raised by a single parent in a public housing project in Birmingham, Alabama. I was keenly aware of living in and through the "urban nightmare."

Everyday 1,118 black teenagers are victims of violent crimes; 1,451 black children are arrested; and 907 black teenage girls get pregnant. A generation of black males is drowning in its own blood in prison camps that we euphemistically call "inner cities." And things are likely to get worse. Some forty years after the beginning of the Civil Rights Movement, younger African Americans are now growing up unqualified even for slavery.

By God's grace, in and through the love and determination of our mother (Momma Syl), we were all able to go on to college and emerge from the entrapment of poverty. Through much prayer and hard work, we began to distance ourselves from the community of the economically, educationally, and socially disenfranchised to what I call "Buppieville" (Black Urban Professionals).

It is important to remember God's word to the Israelites after they were leaving the bondage of Egypt, "Don't forget how you got over." My soul looked back and remembered how my family "got over." God began to tug at my heart, which caused me to reexamine my attitude toward the *community of need.*

Through his Word, God showed me a new answer to the question "Who is my neighbor?" In Luke's Gospel, Jesus tells the parable of the good Samaritan (Luke 10:25–37) to shock everyone who hears it, because this parable identifies your neighbor as *anyone in need.* A good neighbor is anyone of any race or social background who inconveniences himself or risks his reputation for someone in need. The needs of others tend to bring out various *attitudes* in all of us. In the story of the good Samaritan, Jesus makes it very clear which attitude is acceptable to him. If we are honest, we will find ourselves in the place of the lawyer in Luke 10, needing to learn again who our neighbor is.

In verse 25, Jesus is approached by a lawyer, an expert in the Jewish law. The lawyer was not seeking the truth. He was not really trying to discover the way to God; his goal was to discredit Jesus. His hope was that Jesus would respond with an answer that would arouse the people against Jesus. Note: His question to Jesus was about achieving eternal life. *"What must I do?"*(NRSV, emphasis mine) The lawyer obviously had an assumption that he had some role to play in achieving eternal life.

Inherent in the lawyer's question is a major problem of our day: *radical individualism.* This leads to the humanistic philosophies that say, "I am in control of my life and destiny." To the lawyer, eternal life was by individual efforts (works). Many people today think that somehow we can be "good enough." The lawyer had no concept of God's love and grace in his salvation plan (Eph. 2:4–8; Titus 3:5–7).

Francis A. Shaeffer, in his book *How Shall We Then Live,* defines two impoverished values that grow out of this radical individualism: (1) personal peace, which means just to be let alone, not to be troubled by the troubles of other people whether across the world or across the city; the goal is to live one's life with a minimal possibility of being disturbed; and (2) affluence, which means an ever-increasing prosperity, a life made up of things and more things; success is judged by an even higher level of material abundance.

In verse 26, the lawyer asked a bottom-line question and Jesus responded with a bottom-line question: You've read the Scriptures; you've been through the catechism, Baptist Training Union, Sunday school; you've been to seminary. You tell me!

Then the lawyer straightened up his bow tie and cleared his throat. Then he opened his little leather box called a "phylactery" which all experts of the law carried on them. Several passages of Scripture were in the box, two of which were from Deuteronomy. The lawyer quoted these two verses from Deuteronomy with confidence: "You shall love the Lord your God with all your heart, and with all your soul, and with all your strength, and with all your mind; and your neighbor as yourself" (Luke 10:27 NRSV).

God's Word is so clear concerning eternal life that we are without excuse. We can have a personal relationship with God who brings about reconciliation both vertically and horizontally. Only an almighty, loving God can enable persons who are dead in their trespasses and sins to know such possibilities.

Can't you see Jesus clapping his hands, "You have answered correctly" (Luke 10:28 NIV). The Greek word for *correctly* is *orthos,* from which our word *orthodox* comes. It means to think correctly, in the proper way. In other words, Jesus said, "You've got the right words, man!"

I am convinced that the church in America has a credibility problem. We claim to have a high view of Scripture. In fact, of the 230 million Americans, 60 million profess to know Christ as their personal Savior. According to these numbers, we should be having a tremendous impact on our neighbors.

We know how to say it!

We know how to sing it!

We know how to dance it!

We know how to meet about it!

In verse 28, Jesus said, *"Just do it!"*

• Love is an active experience, not inactive and dormant.

• Love acts by showing and demonstrating itself.

• Love causes us to discover our real neighbors.

• Love causes us to obey and live eternally.

This is what God's Word says: "We know that we have passed from death to life, because we love the brethren" (1 John 3:14 NKJV). "Owe no one anything except to love one another, for he who loves another has fulfilled the law" (Rom. 13:8 NKJV).

The lawyer sensed that Jesus was saying that he had not fulfilled the Law; he had failed to love his neighbor. So he asked a logical question, "Who is my neighbor?" I want you to turn to someone, or go to your mirror and ask yourself the same question, "Who is my neighbor?"

In the parable of the good Samaritan, Jesus sets forth three principles that are essential to discovering who our neighbor is: (1) admit (v. 29), (2) commit (vv. 30–35), and (3) submit (vv. 36–37).

Admit

The lawyer's inquiry, "Who is my neighbor?" reveals a lack of love. We must *admit* that separatism, racism, classism and, in some parts of the world, tribalism exists. We must *admit* that we sometimes have problems responding to some people because they are different from us.

W. E. B. DuBois, one of our greatest African-American writers, once said, "I still think today as yesterday that the color line is a great problem of this century. But today I see more clearly than yesterday that at the back of the problem of race and color lies a greater problem, which obscures and implements it. And that is the fact that so many civilized persons are willing to live in comfort even if the price of this is poverty, ignorance, and disease of the majority of their fellow men; that to maintain this privilege men wage war, until today war tends to be continuous and universal and the excuse for this war continues to be color, race, classism and separation."

The only way the lawyer could get out of this would be to limit the extent of the command "to love our neighbor" by devaluing his fellow human beings. In the Dred Scott decision of 1857, the Missouri Supreme Court ruled that former slave Dred Scott could not sue the state of Missouri for his freedom. The reason he could not sue was because he was not a "full citizen," and therefore was not able to receive due process of law.

There are differences in ethnicity and culture, as John's vision of the heavenly hosts reveals. In Revelation 7:9 John saw a great host of people from all nations, tribes, peoples, and languages standing before the Lord of glory giving praise to his name. This passage implies that God will be glorified in our cultural and ethnic diversities. Praise God! There are differences but the differences don't make a difference—or they should not make a difference.

In discovering who our neighbor is, we must understand that the evil of racism, separatism, classism, and tribalism perpetuates itself in three ways:

Actively. This is the most obvious of the three and includes such groups as the KKK, the radical faction of the Black Muslims (who claim white people are the devil), and the Neo-Nazis (who claim that blacks, Jews, and all other non-whites are inferior).

Passively. This is the most subtle of the three. Christians sit idly listening to racist jokes, never defending or upholding the offended. We must understand that neutrality always benefits the oppressor. There are well-meaning statements like "I don't see people as black or white." One can infer from this statement that if I saw them as black or as white or any other shade than my own, I might have to deal with them. So therefore, I'll put on my rose-colored glasses and ignore the reality of race, culture, or any other differences. Our silence indicts us as unwilling to face the challenge that differences are real and beautiful when they line up with the standard of God's Word.

Institutionally. This is a system that prohibits access based on race, class, and social status. So often people in public and community life who are different from us are marginalized, categorized, redlined, and eliminated from any real access to the American dream of "justice for all."

The message of the gospel is both redemptive—"Love the Lord with all of your heart"—and relational—"Love your neighbor as yourself." Our responsibility is to demonstrate the power of the whole gospel. The world will know that we are Christians because we have love for the brethren.

Imagine 60 million people saying the right words, singing the right songs, shouting the right shout, but having very little influence in transforming culture with the values of the kingdom. Perhaps this is why our churches are losing 2.7 million members per year to secularism and nominalism.

Commit

We must also commit ourselves to loving our neighbors by acting responsibly. We do not need welfarism; we need empowerment at the grassroots level. Many people are hurting in our society, and we must be intentional in our response to those in need. This parable reveals various attitudes toward those who are in need of our love.

- To the lawyer, the wounded was a subject to discuss.
- To the thieves, the wounded was an opportunity to exploit.
- To the religious, the wounded was a problem to avoid.
- To the innkeeper, the wounded was a customer to serve for a fee.
- To the Samaritan, the wounded was a human being worth being cared for and loved.

My question: Who are the wounded to you today? The wounded are precious in the sight of God.

Longfellow the poet could take a worthless sheet of paper,

write a poem on it, and make it worth $6,000—that's genius. Rockefeller the millionaire could sign his name to a piece of paper and make it worth a million dollars—that's wealth. A painter can take a 50-cent piece of canvas, splash color on it, and make it worth $10,000—that's art. But God can take a worthless, sinful life, wash it in the blood of Christ, put his Spirit in it, and make it a blessing to humanity—that's salvation! I say, glory, glory, hallelujah!

We must commit ourselves to loving our neighbors. The Lord wants us to see that:

• Love is not limited by its object.
• Love is demonstrated by action.
• Love must be intentional.
• Love will cost you something.

It cost the Samaritan his clothes, wine, oil, transportation, money, and time.

Submit

Finally, we must submit to God's command to love. The question our Lord asked forces the lawyer to a decision, to recognize that our neighbors are often people different from us.

Note that in verse 37 of our text the lawyer had difficulty even saying the word *Samaritan*. He replied, "The one who had mercy on him" (NIV). But he could not avoid the truth the Lord had revealed through this parable. Today, we cannot avoid the truth that our neighbors are people created in the image of God who are different from us and therefore must be loved not only by God but also by those who claim to know God.

There is something about the love of God in our hearts that causes us to respond to our neighbors. The supreme validation of our relationship to God is our love for our neighbors. There is no place for prejudice, favoritism, or insensitivity in the family of Christ. We who have been born again through faith in the Lord Jesus Christ are equals in God's sight. And that equality should be evident in the way we treat others.

A man attended a church regularly for several months, but he was always ignored. His clothes were old and worn, and the people tended to avoid him. Because they knew nothing about him, no one ever spoke to him. One Sunday as he took a seat in church, he intentionally left his hat on. As the pastor stood on the platform and looked over the audience, he noticed the man with the hat right away. Beckoning to one of the deacons, the pastor asked him to go tell the man that he forgot to remove his hat. When the deacon spoke to the man, he responded with a big smile and said, "I thought that would do it. I have attended this church for six months, and you are the first person who has talked to me."

• How do we treat people who are different than we are?
• Who is your neighbor today?
• What is your responsibility in discovering your neighbor?

The world will know that we are Christians when we begin to be good neighbors. Partiality builds walls; love breaks them down.

Chapter 8

When You Show Partiality

FRANK M. BARKER JR.

James 2:1–13

The Context of This Sermon

I grew up in Birmingham, Alabama, in a Christian home but went the way of all flesh until as a Navy jet fighter pilot in the midst of close calls, I began to think seriously about the meaning of life and the folly of resisting God. In seeking to follow him, I felt called to the ministry. After the military I went to seminary, only to discover I was not really a Christian in that I had totally missed the fact that salvation is a gift through trusting in Christ alone, not by improving my record.

Upon graduation from seminary in June 1960, I was

FRANK M. BARKER JR. is pastor emeritus of Briarwood Presbyterian Church in Birmingham, Alabama, a congregation he founded and has served faithfully for forty years. After graduating from Auburn University in 1953, Barker served four years as a jet pilot in the United States Navy. He holds two degrees from Columbia Theological Seminary and an honorary doctoral degree from Reformed Theological Seminary. Dr. Barker has served as moderator of the General Assembly of the Presbyterian Church in America. Under his leadership, Briarwood Presbyterian Church became one of the largest congregations in the PCA, noted for its emphasis on personal evangelism, Christian discipleship, and world missions. His writings include A Living Hope, Encounters with Jesus, *and* 1 Timothy: Pure Heart, Good Conscience, Sincere Faith. *Dr. Barker first preached this sermon from James during the height of racial strife in Birmingham in the 1960s. His commitment to racial reconciliation, forged in the crucible of social conflict and revolutionary change, has continued to shape his ministry and personal witness.*

called to start a new church in Birmingham, Alabama. Birmingham was a hotbed of racial division with race riots, police dogs, fire hoses, burning crosses, and children killed when the Sixteenth Street Baptist Church was bombed. African Americans were visiting white churches in groups and, in many cases, they were being turned away. I was asked to speak at one church across town, and the pastor took me out in the lobby and showed me the clubs his deacons planned to use to beat off any blacks who tried to enter their church. Our church officers had made a decision that any such visitors would be welcomed, but we knew there were people in our congregation with strong misgivings about integration. We had made no real effort to reach out to the African-American community.

At this point I had started preaching through the Book of James. I had finished chapter 1, and in the midst of the next week I had an experience that marked a turning point in my ministry and the church's ministry in this area. When I had the experience (described in the following sermon), I really had not thought about the content of the James passage for the coming Sunday. As I began to work on the sermon . . . well, you decide about what we Presbyterians call "God's providential dealings with us."

This sermon as recorded here is pretty much as I preached it on June 21, 1968. Some of the terms, such as *colored*, are dated. While I don't want to offend, I felt it best to use the original version.

The Theme of James

James is concerned with the practical result or fruit of our faith. In the first chapter he cautions about the danger of being a hearer but not a doer of the Word and deceiving ourselves. "Pure religion and undefiled [real Christianity] before God . . . is this, To visit the fatherless and widows in their affliction, and to keep himself unspotted from the world" (v. 27). It is in acts of

genuine love and kindness, and in resistance to conforming to
the world's value system, that a genuine relationship with Jesus
Christ is demonstrated.

In the second chapter James continues the theme of the folly
of any profession of Christianity that doesn't manifest itself in
right behavior toward our fellowman. He strongly condemns the
evil of "showing respect of persons": "My brethren, have not the
faith of our Lord Jesus Christ, the Lord of glory, with respect of
persons" (v. 1).

"Respect of persons" means to show favoritism or partiality.
As the Amplified New Testament puts it, "My brethren, . . .—
show no prejudice, no partiality. Do not [attempt to] hold and
practice the faith of our Lord Jesus Christ . . . together with—
snobbery!"

An Illustration of It in the Light of Our Own Situation (vv. 2–4)

By way of explanation James gives an illustration: "If there
come unto your assembly a man with a gold ring, in goodly apparel, and there come in also a poor man in vile raiment; And ye
have respect to him that weareth the gay clothing, and say unto
him, Sit thou here in a good place; and say to the poor, Stand
thou there, or sit here under my footstool: Are ye not then partial in yourselves, and are become judges of [with] evil
thoughts?"

Or as Phillips translates it, "Doesn't that prove that you are
making class-distinctions in your mind, and setting yourselves
up to assess a man's quality?"—a very bad thing.

James could have used other examples. As a minister, I am
on occasion tempted to show partiality within the church.
When I preach on sins that are particularly practiced by the
more influential of the congregation, I may feel, *Had not I better tread lightly on this?* Sometimes a man might be elected to

church office because of his position in society and not because of his walk with the Lord. In the area of evangelistic efforts, if we spend more effort on evangelizing one group within society but neglect another, we are showing partiality.

This principle has obvious implications for every Christian today as we try to demonstrate the reality of our faith in the pressing problems of social and racial relations. This very obviously applies to segregation within the church. What is that except making a difference between people, showing partiality?

How does our church measure up in the light of that? Our General Assembly has consistently condemned any distinction between the races within the church. Our presbytery has consistently enforced that and has consistently, emphatically supported the fact that racial distinction within the church is wrong. And the session, the ruling body of this congregation, has also said that there should be no distinction made, that people are to be treated as equals within our congregation. This was done years ago.

And so, officially, we examine ourselves and we say we are all right. But practically, are we? Honestly, are we? What about this matter of our evangelistic efforts? Do we make a distinction here? Do we not labor to bring in one class and overlook others? We have in our own immediate area a poverty stricken group. We call them "Slab Town." The name indicates the poverty and despair. And have we made an honest effort over the years to reach into that situation evangelistically? I don't think we have.

Then there is the colored population. Have we sought to evangelize them? I had this brought home to me in a rather sharp way this week as I visited a colored patient in a colored, Catholic hospital at the request of one of our members. The patient, a young man, is paralyzed from his neck down. As I walked into the room there were a number of other young black men standing around talking with him. When I introduced myself as a minister, there was immediate interest. And, as I began to talk to this young man about Christianity, there was lively participation by the others present. One particular young man began to take the lead in the conversation. He was a very militant, anti-church, anti-Christian, anti-white young Negro. He was very articulate as he argued against the white man and what he called "the white man's religion."

As the debate continued, a crowd gathered. In the middle of the debate one young orderly who had been listening asked me, "Are you the pastor of the church or the assistant pastor?"

I said, "I'm the pastor."

"Do you preach brotherly love?"

I said, "I certainly hope that I do." And as I said it, I cringed because I feared what was coming next.

"How many colored people are there in your congregation?"

"None," I said. I wanted to say, *But they're welcome! Our doors are open!* But I didn't say that because I thought, *Suppose, as I say that, twenty-odd of these fellows come Sunday? Am I prepared for that? Are my people prepared for that? Is that really what I want?*

Right there I lost the debate! "Yeah—Christianity! Sure—brotherly love!"

Have we not been partial? Have we not been guilty of this thing that James condemns? I have.

The Injustice of It in the Light of the Issues (v. 4)

Notice that James points out the *injustice* of such partiality when he says: "Are ye not then partial in yourselves, and are become judges of evil thoughts?"

Have we not made a difference? In making that difference, did you not do wrong? Does not your own conscience convict you? This is James's appeal to us. Think of the injustice of it in the light of the issues involved. Think of what is at stake, the eternal salvation of souls. We believe this. We believe that if a person doesn't come to a true knowledge of Jesus Christ as the Son of God who died for our sins and rose from the dead through someone explaining the gospel in a way that he can understand, and then challenging him, and God opening his heart, that person is eternally doomed. I know that we are tempted to say, "They have their churches and they wouldn't be at home here." But we don't treat others that way. We do everything we can to reach them and make them feel welcome.

How often does our visitation group go out and in visiting with a family someone will say to them, "Well, we visited such and such a church and the people just were not friendly so we didn't go back there." Suppose they not only were not friendly but they were actively hostile and you could feel the hostility? Do you think that would be a stumbling block to someone who is searching for Christ?

I read about a chauffeur who was driving a couple across the desert section of our nation back when cars first came on the market. Something went wrong with the car and they were stranded in the desert. He tried to repair it but was not successful and, as no cars came by, there was no way to get help. The couple sat in the car and waited. A day rolled by. Two days came and went. Periodically the chauffeur would look under the hood and tinker around but couldn't seem to get the car to run. At the end of the week, the couple died. Someone came along and the chauffeur was found to be in relatively good health. He had been drinking water out of the radiator. He was charged with murder because there was plenty of water for all three and he didn't share it with the other two. He was found guilty. Will not God find us guilty of the injustice of not sharing the Water of Life with our brothers and sisters right at hand?

The Inconsistency of It in the Light of Your Profession and God's Action (vv. 5–6a)

James not only brings out the injustice of such partiality but also the *inconsistency* of it in the light of our profession and of God's action. Our profession is that we believe that the true riches are those that Jesus Christ gives, spiritual riches. "Hearken, my beloved brethren, Hath not God chosen the poor of this world rich in faith, and heirs of the kingdom which he hath promised to them that love him? But you have despised the poor."

We profess to believe that the thing that makes a person rich is his or her faith in Jesus Christ. If a person has accepted Christ's claim to be God the Son, and that he went to the cross to pay for our guilt, and then this person places his trust in Christ alone for his salvation and submits his will to Christ, that person is wealthy! The thing that really distinguishes one person from another is not the color of his skin or the amount of money he has, but whether he has by faith entered the kingdom of God. This is the thing that divides mankind into two great groups.

We profess that, and yet is not our action inconsistent with our profession if we are partial, if we distinguish on some other basis? Isn't it inconsistent in the light of God's action? "Has not *God* chosen these?" says James. If God has received them, who am I to withhold in any way a full and hearty welcome? If the president of your company receives a man and wants him welcomed and you are hostile or shut the door in his face, where then do you stand with the president? You wouldn't dream of doing that; it would be inconsistent. And how inconsistent is it when God has received a person for me to withhold reception?

God says that he is not willing that any should perish. Christ preached the gospel to the poor, and he crossed the racial barrier and preached to the Samaritans. He told his disciples to evangelize all. His last words prior to his ascension were, "Ye shall be witnesses unto me both in Jerusalem, . . . in Samaria" (Acts 1:8). Samaria? Remember the Jews had no dealings with the Samaritans. That was like saying, "Start your evangelism among the colored population of the city." We are inconsistent if we send missionaries to Africa (which we do, praise God!) and don't seek to evangelize our own area.

The Illogic of It in the Light of the World Situation (vv. 6b–7)

James says to practice such discrimination is not only to be guilty of injustice and inconsistency but also it is *illogical*. Consider the illogic of it in the light of the world situation. He says, "Do not rich men oppress you, and draw you before the judgment seats? Do not they blaspheme that worthy name by the which ye are called?"

James reminds his readers of what is actually happening in the world. In the light of the opposition of the wealthy to Christianity, does your behavior make sense?

Need I remind you and myself of what is going on in America? The revolution, the violence in the streets is going on! Oh, we've got a breather until next summer. Do you think next summer will be any worse than last summer? You know it will. Do you think the government is going to stop it? You know it won't. What do you think can stop it? Only God. Do you think God will stop it if his people who call themselves by his name are inconsistent and unwilling to do as he commands? Doesn't God normally use means when he changes something? Doesn't he normally use someone in a situation through whom he works?

Do you carry insurance on your home? On your life? Why? You're concerned about your family. That is the type of appeal James is making. It's illogical to carry insurance because you're concerned about your family and not to give all you've got and are to try to solve this racial problem. If we can't rise any higher than the motive of saving our own hides and the hides of our children, we still would have adequate motive to do it. It is illogical not to do that!

The Illegality of It in the Light of Scripture (vv. 8–11)

Next James brings before us the *illegality of such partiality*: "If ye fulfil the royal law according to the scripture, Thou shalt love thy neighbour as thyself . . . ; But if ye have respect to persons, ye commit sin, and are convinced of the law as transgressors" (vv. 8–9).

God's law says we are to love our neighbor as ourselves. This is the standard Christians are to live by. Christ told the parable of the good Samaritan in answer to the question: "Who is my neighbor?" He told it to a man who was seeking to justify himself in not loving his neighbor. In the parable, Christ has a Samaritan cross a racial and religious barrier to help a Jew. He says, in effect, that commandment means that you seek to meet your fellow man's need regardless of his social status or race. If he has a need and you can meet it, love requires that you do so at your expense and risk. To discriminate is to break the royal law!

The plea that we have obeyed in other areas is not acceptable. I'm tempted to enter that plea. I'm tempted to say, "Well, Lord, we've worked hard in reaching people for you. And we've been faithful. We stood up for the truth. Think of all we've done right."

That plea won't be accepted. Look at verses 10 and 11: "For whosoever shall keep the whole law, and yet offend in one point, he is guilty of all. For he that said, Do not commit adultery, said also, Do not kill." (And he also said, "Do not show partiality.") "Now if thou commit no adultery, yet if thou kill, thou art become a transgressor of the law."

The law is one. We cannot pick and choose: "We will obey nine and omit the tenth." The lawgiver is One. To pick and choose is to set myself in opposition to him. The fact that we have learned to obey in other areas means that we have learned to walk in the light and have received more light. To disobey here is to go very clearly against light. To whom much is given, much shall be required. Our very adequacy or maturity is the thing that makes us so guilty.

The problem of race was one of the earliest the church faced. Jesus commanded them to go into all the world, but the Jewish Christians wouldn't cross over to the Gentiles until God so dealt with Peter that he had no choice but to go to the house of Cornelius. We read the story and are amazed that Peter could have been so thickheaded. And then we do the very same thing. When Peter was called on the carpet by the Jewish church, he described how God had dealt with him and said, "Who was I that I could withstand God?" (Acts 11:17 NKJV). So they crossed that barrier at great risk. It could have brought severe persecution from members of their own race, who were offended at this. It could have rendered further witness to their fellow Jews ineffective if not impossible.

You pick this up when Paul addresses his fellow Jews in Jerusalem and they listen to him until he brings in the race issue, until he says, "And God sent me to the Gentiles" (Acts 22:21). At that they stopped their ears and tried to kill him. It was a very risky undertaking, but they did it. They did it because they had to obey God rather than their own likes and dislikes.

The Importance of It in the Light of Judgment Day (vv. 12–13)

The final argument that James makes is the importance of this in the light of the fact that we must give account to God one day: "So speak ye, and so do, as they that shall be judged by the law of liberty. For he shall have judgment without mercy, that hath showed no mercy; and mercy rejoiceth against judgment" (vv. 12–13).

Notice the certainty of judgment. Every person will have to stand before the judgment seat of Christ and give account for the things done in the body, whether good or evil (2 Cor. 5:10). Note the standard of all judgment, the law of liberty. It is called the law of liberty because Christians know that God in his mercy has through Christ delivered them from the penalties attached to their past disobedience. Through their union with him, his liberating power is at work in them to enable them to obey. So I can't plead, "Lord, I didn't have the resources, the power to do anything about it."

When Christ described the last great judgment where all nations will be gathered before him and he will separate them, as sheep from goats, the basis of division is: "I was a stranger, and ye took me in: . . . in prison, and ye came unto me. . . . Inasmuch as ye have done it unto one of the least of these my brethren, ye have done it unto me" (Matt. 25:35–36, 40).

That is not to say that a person will be saved by his good deeds. Rather, true salvation—a changed heart—will evidence itself in genuine concern for my fellowman. A person who was not merciful to his fellowman can expect no mercy in that great day. "Blessed are the merciful: for they shall obtain mercy"(Matt. 5:7). Brethren, it is no trifling sin that James dwells on so hard and long here. This thing of showing partiality is very serious!

Conclusion

Well then, what shall we do about this?

First, let's be penitent. Let's repent. Let's acknowledge our failure. I acknowledge my failure as your leader. Let's be honest and open with God and with ourselves.

Second, let's pray. Let's pray that God will show us his will for us, how to act in this desperate situation. I read of a church in Cleveland, Ohio, in a downtown situation with the neighborhood changing. While other churches were moving out to the suburbs, this church decided to stay and to look to God to guide them. That church has done a fantastically effective job in reaching colored people. God will guide us as a church and as individuals if we will pray and look to him and be open to his guidance.

Third, let's propagate. Let's propagate the gospel of Jesus Christ as a church and as individuals to everyone, irrespective. Let's seek opportunities to do that. I know that many of you feel this way. I just recently visited in the home of one of our young couples, and they told of how they felt a strong desire to just go to a colored section of town and then go door to door seeking to share their faith. Let's look for opportunities in every contact we have with the colored and in places like Slab Town. You have contacts in one way or another. Let's reach out to them, share the gospel, and invite them to church.

In the midst of my disappointment in my experience in the hospital room that I described earlier, there was one bright spot. After the crowd drifted out, the man in the bed next to the young paralyzed man called me over. He said, "I believe what you said about Christ is true and I would like to become a Christian. How do I do that?" I was able to lead him to Christ. Praise God. I believe amidst all our fears and bumbling, God will bless if we will just tackle this thing.

I don't know the best way to reach out to the black community, but I believe God will guide us if we are serious. If you are interested in giving leadership to such an effort, speak to me following the service today and we will put together a committee and start working on this.

On the other hand, it could be that you are here today and identify with the man in the hospital bed. From what you have heard today or before, and in spite of the inconsistencies of Christians and questions you may have, you basically believe Christ is who he claims to be and you would like to become a Christian. You can do so now if you will surrender to him as your Master and place your trust in him as your Savior. If you would like to do that, pray in your heart after me. "Lord Jesus, I acknowledge my sin and I thank you for dying for me. I do receive you as my Master, purposing to obey you, and I trust You to forgive my sins as a gift and come and live in me. Amen."

Addendum

Following this sermon about fifteen people came up and said they would like to be part of a committee to work on this. We began to meet and pray and ask, "How can we begin to reach out?" The idea came to us of renting a camp and running a week of camp for inner-city youth. As far as we knew, there was no camp available to them. Also we needed a young black man to work with us. The next week the presbytery met and a young black man just out of the Marine Corps who had been involved with the Navigators, a strong parachurch ministry, came before the presbytery as a candidate for the ministry. I asked him to postpone his plans to start college until the fall and work with us in a summer-long program of outreach. He agreed and we were able to rent the presbytery camp. He was a Pied Piper and soon had six different youth groups!

Our committee named our program "Operation New Pace" and had luncheons where we challenged our members to sponsor kids for the camp. Our people as well as some African-American pastors became counselors. From this point, relationships were built with both families and churches. In 1971 we received our first African-American member, Lois Coleman, who had come to Christ through her involvement with

Operation New Pace. She later went on to found Grace House, a ministry in Birmingham for young African-American women who need a home.

About that time we hired our first full-time black staff person to head this ministry. He had come to Christ through one of our ladies, and we had been able to help him attend Columbia Bible College. As time has gone on, we have been able to partner with a number of inner-city churches and parachurch ministries. Our most recent step is to call a gifted and godly African-American assistant minister to give leadership to this aspect of ministry. There is so much that still needs to be done, but, praise be to God, at least we are moving in the right direction!

Chapter 9

Obsessed with the Obvious

ALVIN O. JACKSON
John 4:24

I want to contend that glory can be found in the commonplace. Wisdom can be found in the unexpected and spirituality in the presence of the seemingly unholy. A lot of people are going to miss God while looking for the holy place. And a lot of others are going to miss a lot of glory waiting for the mountain, not knowing it is not the place in which you find yourself, but it is how you are yourself. It's not your position; it's your condition. It's not where you are; it's who's there. If I have a right spirit, if I have permitted my heart to be contrite, God can give me a better time passing through the alley than some folk can have standing in the pulpit. Some folk are going to miss the joy of living

ALVIN O. JACKSON is senior pastor of National Christian City Church in Washington, D.C. A native of Laurel, Mississippi, Dr. Jackson holds degrees from Butler University (B.A.), Duke Divinity School (M.Div.), and United Theological Seminary (D.Min.). For nearly twenty years, Dr. Jackson served as pastor of the Mississippi Boulevard Christian Church in Memphis, Tennessee. During his ministry there, this congregation grew from a participating membership of 350 to one of more than 7,800, making it the largest and fastest-growing congregation of the Christian Church (Disciples of Christ) in North America. During his long pastoral tenure in Memphis, and now from his historic pulpit in Washington, Dr. Jackson models a ministry of reconciliation across racial and denominational divides. Through his preaching and pastoral work, he projects a winsome, compelling witness for the gospel of God's grace, which calls all persons to new life in Jesus Christ.

waiting for the high mountain, not knowing you can do some great things in a valley.

Here is a simple story that contains a profound truth and illustrates the danger of being obsessed with the obvious. There was a man who had seven children. His wife had given her life in the birth of the last child. The man was left with the children to raise. The family lived out in the wide open countryside. And on one particular day six of the children had gone away with friends and only the baby was left behind. The father needed to go into town to take care of some business. The baby was asleep so he called the dog, a rottweiler.

The dog had been in the family for years. They had raised it from a pup. He decided to leave the baby with the dog. He said to the dog, "As you have acted in the past, act again. Let no harm come to the baby." He talked to the dog as if the dog understood what he was saying. He left with a sense of assurance, knowing that the dog had been trusted before and so why not trust him now? Seconds lost their identity in minutes. Minutes were swallowed up by several hours.

The moment came when the man started home again. The closer he got to home, he began to feel a kind of restlessness and uneasiness but could not fix the reason why. And so he pressed upon the accelerator, and when he got to the open gate of the house, there was a strange quietness, an eeriness. He made his way to the house and saw the baby's bassinet lying on its side with the little mattress and the sheet in disarray. He looked and saw some blood, followed it off the porch and into the yard. He looked for the child, but he could not find the baby. His heart sank. He panicked. His mind was playing tricks on him.

The man ran hurriedly around the house and saw the dog sitting there with blood on its mouth, licking its paw. Blood on its teeth and no baby! He began to chide himself. *I should have known better, loyal though he has been. Dependable in the past. But I should have known that he is just a dog! I should not have left the baby with this dog!* So he rushed into the house, got his shotgun, and ran back out and looked at the dog. With tears in his eyes, he loaded both barrels and let the dog have it.

The dog rolled over and looked up at him with a look that seemingly tried to communicate something, but he loaded the gun again and let him have it a second time. The dog rolled over dead. He went to the porch and sat down with his head in hand, took the little mattress from the bassinet, and held on to it and continued to cry and chide himself. *I should have known better,* he said over and over to himself.

Then a voice, a cry, split through the silence. He identified the sound as a child. He jumped up and ran into the house, got on his knees, and looked under the bed and there was the baby! The baby had been awakened from his sleep by the noise. He got on his stomach and pulled the baby out and held on to him and kissed him. In his happiness and relief, he had forgotten. He looked out and saw the gun on the porch, ran in the back yard, and there was the dog claimed by death.

He went back and did what he should have done in the beginning. He followed the trail of blood into the yard, and beyond the yard into the grass. He looked down and found a dead wolf that had come down out of the mountains. Evidently its hunger had brought it near the house. When the dog saw the wolf, he had fought the wolf on the porch and the movement had knocked the bed over and the baby had crawled into the house in fear. The dog had fought the wolf in the yard, beyond the yard, into the weeds. And the blood he saw was the dog's own blood he had given protecting the baby.

Running back to where the dog lay, the father started apologizing, saying, "I'm sorry; I had no way of knowing. I saw the blood on your paw and no child. Obviously you had not killed the baby, but I just didn't know!" This man was obsessed with the obvious but he missed the truth!

A simple story, but a profound truth. Is it true? I have no way of knowing. I'm not interested in its authenticity. I'm not even concerned about that dog. There's something here much deeper than a man killing a dog. There is something here that not only shakes the foundations of time, but troubles eternity. My mind goes back some two thousand years ago. There was a baby born in Bethlehem. He came into the world to save it. But because he didn't look like a conqueror, a king of royal blood; because he didn't come in military power and glory; because he didn't act like other proud and arrogant men; because he was born in an obscure village of peasant parents; because he looked like a nobody, we nailed him to a cross. They called him Jesus, but they didn't know who he was. "He came unto his own, and his own received him not" (John 1:11).

I submit that we are obsessed with the obvious—with what the ear can hear, the eye can see, the hand can touch—so obsessed that we miss the real. And our obsession with the obvious is the reason for our racism, sexism, and classism. We put labels on people, we categorize them, we write them off—and we miss the blessing that God would give us through these people. Our minds are already made up; we shut the door with our obsession and miss our blessing.

Such was almost the case in our text. A woman from Samaria almost missed Jesus. John records the encounter between Jesus and this woman of Samaria in the fourth chapter of his Gospel. Jesus and his disciples were traveling from the southern region of Judea to the northern region of Galilee. Rather than taking the long way around, which is what an orthodox Jew would do, they went the direct route through the territory of Samaria and came to Jacob's well.

Jesus and his disciples were thirsty, tired, and hungry.

Having traveled all the way from Jerusalem, Jesus sent his disciples on into the village of Sychar for food while he rested in the shadows of Jacob's well. As he sat there on the edge of the ledge, a woman from the village of Sychar in Samaria came with her water pots to draw water. She made her way cautiously around the stranger seated there. She didn't speak to him, for it would have been inappropriate for a woman to speak to a stranger. And so it was Jesus who initiated the encounter with a simple request. He said to her, "Give me a drink."

The woman responded by saying the obvious. Based upon his physical features, she knew that he was a Jew. She also knew how bitterly the Jews had fought against the Samaritans, partly because of mixed blood, and partly because of an argument on religion dealing with where the people of God should worship. And because of it, the Jews and Samaritans had no dealings with one another. There was deep animosity between them. And so this woman said to Jesus, in essence, "Because of who you are, I am not sure that I ought to respond according to your request. Obviously we ought not be talking with each other!"

The woman answered Jesus the only way she knew, with the defensiveness and prejudice that had been instilled in her from childhood. She said, "How is it that you, a Jew, ask a drink of me, a woman of Samaria? Have you no regard for social standards or historic attitudes? Where is your sense of propriety? Don't you realize that because our people do not get along, we are not supposed to like each other, talk to each other, or relate to one another in any significant way? That much is obvious!"

I am so glad that God is patient with those of us who are obsessed with the obvious, because God realizes that many of us don't know any other way to act. We don't know how to respond in any other way. We have been hurt or rejected. Someone has taken advantage of us. Someone has done us in, and we don't know any other way to be than mean, vengeful, defensive, supersensitive, and distrustful. Black folks and white folks in this country have been at odds for so long that often we don't know how to approach one another initially without suspicion or hostility. We even view as strange those who try to bridge the gap or who refuse to let historic differences between groups determine the character of their personal relationships.

But I am so glad that our God is patient with us. Jesus directed the conversation toward higher things and, in essence, based on John 4:10–18, told the woman, "If you knew the gift of God, and who it is that asks for a drink, then you also would have forgotten about custom and propriety and asked him for a drink and he would have given you living water."

But the woman, pragmatic as she was and still obsessed with the obvious, looked at Jesus and said, "Why, you have nothing to draw with and the well is deep." This woman almost missed her blessing because she was caught up in what she could see—in what she could feel and touch. She didn't understand that there was another realm of reality beyond the visible. Jesus was trying to take the woman to a higher level of living. She was still wrapped up in the physical, the carnal, the mundane, the material, but Jesus was talking about living water! Spiritual water! Finally the woman said, "If what you say is true, give me some of that water that I thirst not and won't have to come here to draw again."

But Jesus knew the woman still hadn't understood. She was still talking about physical water. She still hadn't heard him. And so he took a different approach. He said, "Go call your husband and tell him to come here."

The woman said, "Well, I have no husband."

Jesus said, "Right, but you have had five and the man you are living with is not your husband."

The Samaritan woman had flitted from one marriage to another and one husband to another, whether by choice or circumstance; but after five empty marriages, with her latest man she had finally said, "What's the use of even going through the formality of marriage?" She had just moved in and shacked up with the brother. And so as Jesus confronted this woman, it threw her off. *How does this man know me?* she thought. *He seems to know everything I have done!*

Continuing with verses 19 and 20, however, she quickly recovered her composure and raised a diversionary question. "I see that you are a prophet, a religious person. You know, I have a question about religion that has always bothered me. My Samaritan ancestors have worshiped God here on Mt. Gerizim, and they say that this is the house where God lives, but you Jews say that God lives in your temple on Mount Moriah in Jerusalem. Now tell me, where does God really live? Who is right, the Jews or the Samaritans?"

Hers was a typical response. When Jesus gets close to us and puts his finger on our sin and struggle—when he touches that sensitive spot in our lives—what do we do?

Many of us try to change the subject and evade confrontation with the real issue. We start raising all kinds of intellectual and theological questions. This woman was trying to evade confrontation and avoid Jesus, but Jesus reminded her that God is not a physical person who lives in a physical house on Mount Gerizim or Mount Moriah. God is a spirit and you can't monopolize the spirit on a mountain, and you can't place the spirit in a location. And one denomination can't dominate the spirit. You can't lock the spirit up in the church. You can't just meet the spirit here between 11:00 and 12:00 on Sundays and not run into the spirit any more. You can't box the spirit in or put the spirit between bookends. You can't circumscribe the spirit in a creed. You can't confine or fully define spirit. God is spirit!

And the only way to worship God who is spirit is in spirit. The spirit must worship the spirit. Jesus says to this woman and to us: Don't become obsessed with the obvious. God is spirit. God is bigger than you think!

But he is also saying to this woman and to us: We are spirit; the essence of who we are is spirit. We can be bigger than we think! It's obvious that we are different: male, female, black, brown, and white. That's obvious! Our differences are obvious— different backgrounds, different experiences, different skin colors, different cultures, different languages. But that's not really who we are, at the core, at the center. The essence of who we are is spirit. And so we are more alike than different. That is what Jesus was saying to this woman. That may not be obvious, but that's real!

Yes, we are different, but we are more alike than different. This truth came home to me in an interesting and powerful way the other day. I enjoy Tootsie Roll lollipops. I was driving along the other day enjoying my lollipop and thinking about this sermon, and the lollipop seemed to speak to me. The lollipop said to me, "Alvin, look at me; I'm a lollipop." I had a whole packet of lollipops with me, and they all started speaking to me. One of them said, "I am red." Another said, "I am orange." And another, "I am brown." And another, "I'm purple." And in unison they said, "We come in many different colors, but when you get down past the color, the obvious, at the core, at the center, we are all the same. We all have the same little sweet chocolate core!"

And so I remind us not to become obsessed with the obvious. No matter what the color is, at the core, at the center of things, we are all the same! It's OK to acknowledge, affirm, and appreciate our differences. Thank God that he made us different. It would be a mighty dull and boring world if we were all alike. But don't become so obsessed with your differences that you don't understand that we have a common destiny. We are all children of God. We divide the world into male and female, rich and poor, black and white, people like us and people not like us.

But God simply loves the world. And he calls us who have experienced that love to share it with others.

Fred Craddock tells the story of vacationing one summer in the Smoky Mountains of Tennessee. He and his wife had found a lovely little restaurant at a place called Black Bear Inn. He said they were seated there looking out at the mountains, when this old man with white hair, a Carl Sandburg-looking person, came over and spoke to him. The man said, "You here on vacation?" And they said, "Yes." "Well, what do you do?" Craddock said he was thinking this was none of his business, but he finally said, "I am a minister."

The old man said, "Oh, a minister! Well, do I have a story for you." And he pulled out a chair and sat down, just took a place uninvited, and proceeded to tell his story. Craddock said he found out later that the man was eighty years old and a former governor of Tennessee.

"I was born back here in these mountains," the man said, "and when I was growing up, I attended the Laurel Springs Church. My mother was not married and as you might expect in those days, I was greatly embarrassed about that. At school I would hide in the weeds by a nearby river and eat my lunch alone, because the other children were very cruel. And when I went to town with my courageous mother, I would see the way people looked at me trying to guess who my daddy was. The preacher at the little church fascinated me, but at the same time, he scared me. He had a long beard, a rough-hewn face, a deep voice, but I sure liked to hear him preach. But I didn't think I was welcomed at church so I would go just for the sermon. And as soon as the sermon was over, I would rush out so nobody would say, 'What's a boy like you doing here in church?'

"But one day," the old man said as he continued to tell his story about his boyhood days, "I was trying to get out of the church, but some people had already gotten in the aisle so I had to remain. I was waiting, getting in a cold sweat, when all of a sudden I felt a hand on my shoulder. I looked out of the corner of my eye and realized it was the face of the preacher, and I was scared to death! The preacher looked at me. He didn't say a word, he just looked at me, and then he said, 'Well boy, you're a child of . . .' and he paused. I knew he was going to try and guess not who my mother was but who my father was. The preacher said, 'You're a child of . . . umm. Why, you are a child of God. I see a striking resemblance, boy!' He swatted me on the bottom and said, 'Now go and claim your inheritance.'"

And then the old man who was telling the story said to Fred Craddock, "I was born on that day!"

May you be born this day, for you are a child of God. Now, go claim your inheritance.

Chapter 10
Reconciliation: Our Calling
MAXIE D. DUNNAM
2 Corinthians 5:19

Paul put it clearly in his second letter to the Corinthians, chapter 5, verse 19: "God was in Christ reconciling the world to Himself . . . and has committed to us the word of reconciliation" (NKJV). It is at the heart of what the Christian faith and life are all about—reconciliation.

There was a demonstration of reconciliation in Memphis on the Saturday before Easter and Easter Sunday, 1998. Christ United Methodist, the church of which I was the minister for twelve years, and Mississippi Boulevard Christian Church started an annual Easter service of reconciliation in 1997.

Christ Church is a six-thousand-member predominantly white church. Mississippi Boulevard is an eight-thousand-member

---

MAXIE D. DUNNAM is president of Asbury Theological Seminary. A native of Deemer, Mississippi, he holds degrees from the University of Southern Mississippi (B.S.) and Emory University (Th.M.), and Asbury Theological Seminary (D.D.). A wise and seasoned pastor, Dr. Dunnam has worked for racial reconciliation in the congregations he has served from Georgia to California, including Christ United Methodist Church in Memphis, where he was senior minister for twelve years (1982–1994). A popular speaker and prolific author, he has published more than forty books on evangelism, discipleship, and the Christian life. He has been a senior editor for Christianity Today and currently serves as chairman of world evangelism for the World Methodist Council.

predominantly African-American church. The two congrega-tions had worked together for years in mission and ministry to the city, primarily in the area of housing. They decided to make a dramatic witness and call the city to racial reconciliation. So they planned a joint Easter celebration of worship. Fifteen thousand people of all races came together in the Pyramid, the public arena in downtown Memphis.

The Pyramid is the home of the University of Memphis basketball team. They refer to it as the "Tomb of Gloom" for visiting teams. In that first Easter service of reconciliation, Alvin Jackson, then minister of Mississippi Boulevard, began his sermon with this shout: "We have changed the *Tomb of Gloom* into a *Resurrection arena*. We are saying to this city: In Jesus Christ, 'there is neither Jew nor Greek, there is neither slave nor free, there is neither male nor female; for you are all one in Christ Jesus'" (Gal. 3:28 NKJV).

The next year, 1998, on the Saturday before the second an-nual Easter Celebration of Reconciliation, a second dramatic witness was added. A fifteen-mile human chain from downtown Memphis all the way to Germantown—perhaps twenty-five thousand people, black and white—joined together holding hands to demonstrate the oneness that is ours in Jesus Christ. Placards announced the call of the gospel: "Love your neighbor." Passersby were greeted and invited to the Easter celebration the next day. It was a glorious demonstration of reconciliation.

There is a beautiful illustration of reconciliation in the film *Places in the Heart.* That movie is about life in Waxahachie, Texas, in 1935. It opens with an old familiar hymn tune. That should have given the viewer a hint, but most of us missed it. The sheriff is offering a thoughtful prayer over fried chicken, mashed potatoes, and gravy. His wife catches the young daugh-ter peeking in the midst of the prayer and the older son devoutly praying. As the film unfolds, a drunken young man accidentally kills the sheriff, and the Ku Klux Klan drags the young man to his death.

The sheriff's widow, played by Sally Fields, is named Mrs. Spaulding. The town banker tries to make her sell the forty-acre farm and split her family up among relatives.

The poignancy of the film comes when the widow decides that if she is going to make it, it is up to her and her alone. She takes in a blind World War I veteran, brother-in-law of the banker; gets help from an itinerant black man; picks her cotton crop until her fingers bleed and her back nearly breaks; and wins a special prize of one hundred dollars for producing the first bale of cotton in Ellis County. The Ku Klux Klan beats up Moses, the black man who engineered the victorious crop, and he has to leave town.

But the movie is more than a story about Mrs. Spaulding's struggle to survive. It's the story of the triumph of faith and love; it's the picture of the church. Most people probably missed the meaning of that picture of the church. New York film critics gave the movie high marks except for the last scene, where the picture of the church is so poignantly presented. The pastor is reading from 1 Corinthians 13:1–8: "If I speak with the tongues of men and of angels, but do not have love, I have become a noisy gong or a clanging cymbal" (NASB). Then communion is shared. As the communion elements are passed from person to person, the members say, "The peace of God be with you" to each other. Then an amazing thing happens. The camera follows the plate as it moves down the aisle, each person taking the bread and passing it on to the next. The camera focuses on the faces of those present. It moves from Mrs. Spaulding to her husband. He is there now with his family. At his funeral they had sung, "In the sweet bye and bye, we shall meet on that beautiful shore." What a message by a secular filmmaker. This is the way Christian history will end. This is the way it will be—the communion of saints.

But that's not all. The camera moves to the next person in the pew. It's the man who killed the sheriff. He's right there, beside the sheriff. The sheriff hands him the elements of Holy Communion and speaks "peace," the word of reconciliation. The black drifter, who helped the widow make her farm a success, is also there. The blind man she reached out to and took into her home, he's there. The banker, the conniving one who sought to steal her property, he's there. And the couple whose marriage was nearly split apart by his unfaithfulness—Mrs. Spaulding's sister and her husband—they are there, holding hands as they pass the plate to each other. Everyone is there—reconciled members of the household.

No wonder the New York critics didn't like that last scene. They don't know what Christians know, that we belong to a community that is not of this world, a kingdom "not made by human hands, but eternal in the heavens," the "household of God." Listen to what Paul says: "But now in Christ Jesus you who once were far off have been brought near in the blood of Christ. For he is our peace, who has made us both one, and has broken down the dividing wall of hostility, by abolishing in his flesh the law of commandments and ordinances, that he might create in himself one new man in place of the two, so making peace, and might reconcile us both to God in one body through the cross, thereby bringing the hostility to an end" (Eph. 2:13–16 RSV).

Reconciliation is not just an issue of black and white. It is an issue of husband and wife, of rich and poor, of parent and child. It has to do with education, with teachers and students and parents and teachers, with the kind of public schools we provide our children—whether we are going to have public schools that demand guards to keep weapons out, schools that are the setting for rioting and racial conflict.

Reconciliation has to do with our justice system, with our prisons. Think about it. Who is in jail today? Mostly poor people, mostly black people. And why are they there? Why is a sentence for possessing crack five times higher than for possessing powdered cocaine? Why do we continue to build prisons and use our prisons for punishment rather than rehabilitation? We spend more money on keeping a person in prison for a year than it would cost to send him or her to the best university in the land.

Reconciliation is a lot more than black and white. It is about politicians and how they serve their constituency. It is about bringing our behavior into harmony with our beliefs. It is about what we think of welfare. It is about breaking the cycle of poverty and building a system where welfare will be an emergency measure, not a way of life.

Reconciliation is about the tension in the land our Lord Jesus made holy—tension that breaks out in violence and killing as Jews and Arabs battle for place and power. It's about ethnic cleansing in Bosnia and Kosovo. It is about Christians being persecuted in China.

Reconciliation is about sin and salvation. It's about the cross of Jesus Christ. It's about prodigal children being brought home again.

Reconciliation is God's plan for our salvation and life together. The witness of Scripture is clear: "God was in Christ reconciling the world to Himself" (2 Cor. 5:19 NKJV); "For as many as are led by the Spirit of God, these are sons of God" (Rom. 8:14 NKJV); "Children of God . . . and if children, then heirs; heirs of God and joint heirs with Christ" (Rom. 8:17 NKJV); "There is one body and one Spirit, just as you were called in one hope of your calling; one Lord, one faith, one baptism; one God and Father of all, who is above all, and through all, and in you all" (Eph. 4:4–6 NKJV); "For [Jesus] is our peace, who has made us both one, and has broken down the dividing wall of hostility . . . [reconciling] us both to God in one body through the cross, thereby bringing the hostility to an end" (Eph. 2:14, 16 RSV).

Reconciliation is the bold dream of God . . . a dream that we must ever struggle for, but a dream God guarantees to bring to fruition.

The slaves knew it and sang about it: "I'm gonna sit at the welcomin' table; I'm gonna sit at the welcomin' table; I'm gonna sit at the welcomin' table, one of these days, glory hallelujah, one of these days."

Until that day comes in all its fullness, Christians must carry God's dream in their hearts and allow God to use them to bring that dream to fulfillment in the corner of the world where they live.

So how do we live? What is the source of our power? What is the full dream toward which we move? How do we claim the promise of reconciliation?

First, *we must believe that we are more than we think we are.* One of the reasons the reconciled body of Christ eludes us is that we feel helpless. Racism is such a malignant power. Division between rich and poor is so pronounced. Systems of separation are so entrenched. Selfishness and pride are rampant sins in all our lives. So, we feel helpless. What can one person do?

One of the most fantastic promises of Jesus is in the Gospel of John: "I tell you the truth, anyone who has faith in me will do what I have been doing. He will do even greater things than these, because I am going to the Father" (John 14:12 NIV). Isn't that a breathtaking promise? If this is even remotely possible, then mustn't we admit that we have never taken Jesus seriously? The least we have to confess is that we have certainly been satisfied with far less than he had in mind for us as his followers. So, if we are going to be reconciled, and if we are going to accept the challenge to be ministers of reconciliation, then we need to claim this fantastic promise of Jesus: "Greater things than I have done will you do because I go to the Father."

One of my favorite theologians is Charles Schultz, the artist who provided us the "Peanuts" cartoons. (That ought to tell you something about the kind of seminary president I am!) In one of his cartoon series, he has Snoopy, that hound of heaven, saying to Woodstock, that would-be bird of paradise, "Someday Woodstock is going to be a great eagle." Then in the next frame he says, "He is going to soar thousands of feet above the ground." Woodstock takes off into the air, and as Snoopy looks on, he sees the bird upside down, whirling around crazily. So he has second thoughts. In the third frame Snoopy says, "Well, maybe hundreds of feet above the ground . . ." But hardly have the words gotten out of his mouth when Woodstock plummets to the ground and lies there on his back, looking dazed. Snoopy has to conclude, "Maybe he will be one of those eagles who just walks around." Isn't it amazing how quickly we settle for less than is promised and for less than is possible!

The dramatic power of John 14:12 becomes most pronounced when we keep in mind who said it. Jesus said it—the Man who came to save the world, the Man who forgave and loved and washed his disciples' feet. The Man who made the lame to walk and the blind to see; the Man who calmed the storm and took little children on his lap and blessed them; the Man who ate with sinners and flung his life into the teeth of the raw and rampant prejudice of his day by conversing with the Samaritan woman at the well. The Man who finished all the work God gave him to do, and is now seated at the right hand of the Father, crowned with glory and honor. Can you believe it? That's the Man—Jesus—who said to you and me, "Greater works than these will you do because I go to the Father."

Do we believe it? Do we believe it enough to claim the promise? Our problem is that we trust in Jesus in some things when we need to trust him with all things all of the time. Jesus is telling us, *You are more than you think you are.*

The question is, "How can I believe it? How can I believe that I am more than I think I am?" Think about it. You are important to God. In fact, you are a unique, unrepeatable miracle of God. You have that on the authority of God's Word. Don't you remember Jesus said it? Not even a sparrow falls to the earth without God noticing it, and you are of more value than sparrows. More dramatically, the word is "even the hairs on your head are numbered." It is the witness of Scripture: You are important to God. This means that there is a place in God's heart that only you can fill. God loves each one of us as though each one of us were the only person in the world to love.

Now if it is true, that you are more than you think you are, then know this: your brother, your sister, the black man, the white man, the rich man, the poor man, the prisoner, the person on welfare, and the one who lives on Main Street—if you are more than you think you are, then those around you are more than they think they are. And get this: they are more than you may have thought they were.

There is an old rabbinical story in which the rabbi asked his students, "Children, how can we determine the moment of dawn when the night ends and the day begins?"

One student responded, "When I see the difference between a dog and a sheep?"

"No," said the rabbi.

A second student asked, "Is it when I can see the difference between a fig tree and a grapevine?"

"No."

"Please tell us the answer," begged the students.

The old rabbi responded, "You know the night ends and the day begins when you can look into the face of any human being and have enough light to recognize the person as your brother or your sister, when you can say, 'I see myself in you.' Up until that time it is night, and darkness is still with us."

Well, darkness is still with us, and it will remain with us until we realize that we are more than we think we are, and those around us, those with whom we live, those who live on the other side of the tracks, those whose ways seem strange to us—the night will remain until we realize they, too, are more than they think they are.

So, if we are going to be ministers of reconciliation, we have to claim the promise, "Greater things than I have done will you do because I go to the Father." We have to realize that we are more than we think we are. That being true, those around us are more than we thought they were. They are our brothers and sisters. We have been made one with them through the cross of Jesus Christ.

Now, a second affirmation. *There is something you can be and do but will never be and do apart from Jesus Christ.* I believe that is another part of what Jesus is saying to us. "Greater works than these will you do because I go to the Father"—greater works of reconciliation, greater works of witnessing, greater works of serving, greater works of discipleship. There is something we can be and do but will never be and do apart from Jesus Christ.

Let me make the point by telling you a story. It is a story of reconciliation, but it is also a story that confirms the fact that there is something that we can be and do that we will never be and do apart from Jesus Christ. When I was a pastor in Memphis, one Sunday morning after the worship service I was introduced to a man named Austin Veleff. His wife had been attending our church by herself, but now she introduced this man as her husband. He was then in prison, accused of financial fraud. He had been sent home to Memphis from prison to have surgery and some special medical treatment. His wife brought him to church that morning before he was admitted to the hospital that afternoon. I visited him while he was in the hospital, and, when he returned to prison, he and I began a correspondence. During that time of correspondence we shared deeply with one another, and, of course, I shared the gospel with him.

Gradually the light of Christ dawned in him and he was gloriously transformed.

Two years later, Austin was up for release from prison, first for four months to a halfway house, provided someone would guarantee him a job. He turned to the church. The only job we had at that time was a job that paid a little above minimum salary as a maintenance person. He was delighted to take the job. He went through the halfway house experience, and, as he drew near the end of that time, I kept urging him to look for another job. He refused to do so. Though a college graduate, he was certain God wanted him to stay there, sweeping floors, setting up tables, washing windows.

Austin had been doing that for over a year when I left Christ Church. He wrote me a letter when he heard that I was leaving: "I know you have wanted me to get another job, but I want you to know I have never been happier in my life. Christ has not only freed me from my sins and saved me while I was in prison; he has freed me from my prison of hatred and hostility and bitterness, which had enslaved me and was eating my life away. I am staying here in this minimal job, at least for now, because this church is Christ to me."

Talk about reconciliation, reconciliation to Christ and to life itself. There is more to the story. About six months before I left Christ Church, we started a special ministry called MARRS—Mediation and Restitution/Reconciliation Service. We started that ministry because the courts of Memphis were packed with young men and women, first-time offenders. Nothing good was happening in the system. The people were being punished, but no good thing was happening—no rehabilitation, no healing, no preparation for another kind of life. So we started this ministry, believing that what was needed was not punishment but restitution and reconciliation.

The church invited the courts to sentence the young prisoners to us rather than to prison. We trained counselors, black and white, and put them together in teams to work with these young offenders. The idea was that the offender would have to make restitution for the crime he or she had committed. Perhaps mow the lawn for a month or two for a person from whom he had stolen a television—that kind of thing—some sort of restitution, believing that we do need to pay for our crimes. But also bringing the offender and the one offended face-to-face in order that reconciliation can take place.

You can't imagine the transformation that is taking place as a result of this program. But there is more to the story. Austin Veleff is now the second full-time caseworker in this unique ministry. He wrote me a letter when he had gotten the job, after having worked as a maintenance person at Christ Church until this opportunity came along: "Can you believe it? From prison to Christ, and then to Christ Church. From the maintenance of buildings to the ministry of restitution and reconciliation." Austin is a great witness to the fact that there is something we can be and do but will never be and do apart from Jesus Christ.

The calling is clear. "God was in Christ reconciling the world to himself . . . and has committed to us the work of reconciliation." The fulfillment of that calling is possible when we realize that:

- We are more than we think we are.
- Those around us are more than we thought they were. They are brothers and sisters. We are made one by the cross of Jesus Christ.
- There is a ministry of reconciliation that only we can perform. We can perform it when we claim the possibility that there is something we can be and do but will never be and do apart from Jesus Christ.

Chapter 11

Shattering Wall and Veil

ROBERT SMITH JR.

"And the veil of the temple was rent in twain
from the top to the bottom."
MARK 15:38

"For he is our peace, who hath made both one, and hath
broken down the middle wall of partition between us."
EPHESIANS 2:14

The Jewish temple was a virtual graded construct of separation, separating God from humanity, separating Jew from Gentile, separating male from female. The forefront of the temple construct consisted of the larger court known as the court of the Gentiles, the equivalent of two football fields long. The court of the Jewish women was followed by the court of the Jewish men; then there was the inner court for the Jewish priests, and finally the Holy of Holies.

Draped across the Holy of Holies was a curtain, a veil. It was there for the purpose of creating a distance between deity and humanity. According

ROBERT SMITH JR. is the Professor of Christian preaching at Beeson Divinity School of Samford University. A native of Knoxville, Tennessee, he holds degrees from Cincinnati Bible College (B.S.) and the Southern Baptist Theological Seminary (M.Div.; Ph.D.). For more than twenty years, Dr. Smith served as pastor of the New Mission Missionary Baptist Church in Cincinnati. A popular preacher at national conferences and evangelistic meetings, his sermons have been published in Leadership, Preaching, The Minister's Manual, and The Abingdon Preaching Manual. He is also contributing editor of Preparing for Christian Ministry (1996). This sermon was originally presented at the 1997 annual meeting of the Woman's Missionary Union of the Southern Baptist Convention.

to Flavius Josephus, the ancient historian, once a year the high priest would go beyond this veil to offer up sacrifices for the sins of the people. The Bible certainly reinforces that—there was the sprinkling of the blood of a perfect, spotless lamb on the altar. This veil stood sixty feet in height; it was beautifully, ornamentally decorated with blue, purple, and scarlet colors.

But on this particular occasion, with the commending of the spirit of Jesus, his giving of his last breath to God, God ripped apart the veil. No longer would the high priest need to go in once a year to offer up sacrifices for the sins of people. God in essence was tearing up the mortgage note. Elvina M. Hall took her pen and dipped it in the ink of inspiration and wrote this song when she saw the dramatic, picturesque scene of God tearing up the mortgage note: "Jesus paid it all, all to him I owe. Sin had left a crimson stain; he washed it white as snow."

Paul says when he looks at this text that God has broken down the middle wall of partition. The middle wall of partition was a wall, a barrier that separated the Jewish court from the Gentile court. Once again according to the ancient historian Flavius Josephus, we are told that this middle wall had written alongside it in regular intervals inscriptions that warned the Gentiles of the danger of going beyond the partition. In fact, in 1871, when the temple site was excavated, one such inscription was found. It stated, "No person of another race shall proceed beyond this partition and this enclosed wall about the sanctuary. Any one arrested there will have himself to blame for the penalty of death which shall be imposed as a consequence."

So the purpose of this wall was to keep Jew and Gentile separated. However, when Christ died on the cross and gave his spirit back to God, this wall was shattered. No, not the physical wall; that did not happen until A.D. 70, when the Romans destroyed both the temple and the city. But in essence, in religion, God was shattering the wall, and there was no longer a separation between Jew and Gentile. Hear Paul as he says: "There is neither Jew nor Greek, there is neither bond nor free, there is neither male nor female: for ye are all one in Christ Jesus" (Gal. 3:28).

This veil also signified the fact that it kept at a distance the disclosure of the secret of the mystery of God. It hung there, and as far as the Jews were concerned, it was a symbol of a foreboding presence, a symbol of awe, for no one except the high priest really knew what was behind the veil. Once a year he entered the Holy of Holies, sprinkled the blood on the mercy seat, and stayed there for just a brief period of time. When he came out, the people looked upon him in awe for he had been with God. But when the veil was ripped apart from top to bottom, for the first time the rays of the Syrian sun streamed through, and there was unveiled and revealed for all eyes to see what was behind the Holy of Holies.

And to the surprise of the people, they discovered that God was not there! God could not be concealed. God could not be confined by an inner shrine. God was accessible. God could now be approached directly by individuals, and no longer simply by a high priest. They discovered that God was too big for the Holy of Holies.

In J. B. Phillips's small book *Your God Is Too Small*, he lifts up a caricature that we need to see once again—"God in a box." God is not in a box! God is too big to be contained in a box. He is too big to be contained in our denominational boxes. I used to think that God was a Baptist, and worse than that I used to think that God was a black Baptist. But God is not a Baptist or a Methodist. He is not a white God; he is not a black God; he is not an oriental God. God is God, and God is God because God is God! He's bigger than our boxes, and when the Holy of Holies was revealed, they discovered that God was too big to be confined to that small area. Therefore, the writer to the Hebrews declares, "Let us therefore come boldly unto the throne of grace, that we may obtain mercy, and find grace to help in time of need" (4:16).

That middle wall of partition was a sign of anger for the Gentiles, for some rumors were circulating among the Gentiles. There was a rumor that once a year Jews would take a Gentile behind that forbidden partition, keep him there for a year, fatten him up, and on the great Day of Atonement offer him as a sacrifice. That certainly was not true, for it would have been blasphemous for any Jew to do that. But in the minds of the Gentiles that was a great possibility. In their minds the Jewish people thought they were superior racially, relationally, and religiously. This middle wall of partition that separated the court of the Jews from the court of the Gentiles reinforced that thought.

When Jesus died on that Friday, commending his spirit back to God, the middle wall of partition was shattered. In the Epistle to the Ephesians, Paul reminds us that no longer is there the mystery of the family of God, the mystery that was hidden from the eyes of the prophets, for the family of God now consists of both Jew and Gentile. He says in Ephesians 4:6 that there is "one God and Father of all, who is above all, and through all, and in you all" (NKJV). When he is talking about "all," he is talking about Jewish and Gentile believers alike.

The disaster that we now face is that after two thousand years of knowing that the veil has been torn down, and that the wall has been broken down, in many ways we are still at the same place racially, relationally, and religiously that the Jews were before the wall was torn down and the veil ripped apart. We stand before a torn-down veil attempting to reattach the detached threads and to reweave them into the fabric of a patched-up curtain. We stand before the broken wall making fresh mortar and attempting brick by brick to reassemble the facsimile of a partition.

Brothers and sisters, the wall has been broken down and the veil has been torn down, and they must remain down! It is true, what God has joined together let no one put asunder. *But it is also true that what God has put asunder let no one join together*—the wall is down, the veil has been ripped apart, and it must remain that way.

I heard a story of some soldiers fighting in Europe during World War II. During the combat one of their friends was killed. They wanted to give him a decent burial, so they took him to a nearby cemetery that was adjoined to a church, knocked on the parson's door, and asked the minister if it would be permissible for their comrade to be buried in their cemetery. He said, "I cannot allow that for two reasons. One, the cemetery is reserved for members only, and two, your friend is a foreigner." He denied them access to the cemetery. But he said to them, "I will allow you to bury your friend outside the fence that separates the cemetery from the other part." Well, they did this, and they thanked him for it.

After the war was over, knowing they would not see each other again, they went back to pay their last respects to their friend. They could not find his grave. They knocked on the door of the parson's house. The parson knew who they were, and he knew who they were looking for. He said to them, "The body has not been removed, but I felt bad about denying you access to the cemetery. Although I did not decide to move the body inside the fence, I had the fence moved outward to include your friend."

When I heard that story, I thought, "That's terrific, that's wonderful, that's commendable." But the more I thought about it, I said, "That is not enough." We must not only move the fences outward; we must tear down the fences because fences represent exclusion. It makes no difference how far you move the fences outward; someone is going to be excluded. The fences must be torn down.

Brothers and sisters, we must remember that a fence is always a temptation for someone to move, for we have pharaohs in our churches, pharaohs in our seminaries, pharaohs in our governments, and pharaohs in our school systems who don't know Joseph. As long as we have fences, there is a temptation of moving them back to exclude certain people. We need to tear down the fences! Let the wall remain broken down and let the veil remain ripped apart.

What are we going to do, now that we know the veil has been ripped apart and the wall has been broken down? I think we have to admit that the world needs the church. The world is sick. But worse than that, the church is critically ill. The church needs to be admitted into God's general hospital where it can undergo a period of redemptive observation and have another blood transfusion because a critically ill church cannot minister to a sick world.

We need to see behind the veil. We need to do something once we get beyond the wall. We are blind, but it is not a congenital blindness; it is a self-imposed blindness. None are so blind as those who will not see. Robert F. Kennedy in quoting George Bernard Shaw said, "Some people see things the way they are and ask why. I dream of things the way they could be and ask why not." We must see what is behind the veil. Why don't we see? If we don't see, it's because we don't want to see.

If we see what is behind the veil, it means that we have to accept all human beings as equally human, made in the image of God, a part of the *imago Dei*. Whatever that means, it certainly means that God chose to image himself through us; it certainly means that God chose to communicate to us. We are the only beings that God both listens to and talks to. It certainly means that God intends that we be a community not only with him but with each other. It is impossible for us to love God and not love one another, and it is impossible for us to be in community with God and not be in community with one another.

We often don't want to see what is behind the veil because we don't want to accept each other as equally human regardless of socioeconomic conditions, educational status, and ethnic diversity. We must see each other as fellow humans. If we see what is behind the veil, it often means that we see a reflection of ourselves, and that is always painful. It was George Santayana who said, "He who forgets the past is condemned to repeat it." Often we are perpetuating the mistakes of past generations, and we don't want to see that so we refuse to see what's behind the veil. Maya Angelou, in reflecting upon her abuse as a child that left her a mute for a couple of years, said, "The past despite its wrenching pain cannot be unlived." We cannot erase the past; we cannot ignore the past; we cannot pretend that it never existed. But when faced with courage, it need not be lived again.

We can do something about the present and the future. In a March 6, 1995, article in *Christianity Today,* Billy Graham said, "Racial and ethnic hostility is the foremost social problem that we face today. Just wishing that the problem would go away does not solve the problem. Racial reconciliation must begin with the individual." It is a wonderful thing for denominations to repent. We all need to repent—black, white, red, brown, yellow—it makes no difference. But we don't just need corporate repentance; we need individual repentance. It is easier to stand behind a group, but it is much more difficult for me to say, "*I* need to repent, and I am going to be an ambassador of reconciliation myself!" That's what I see when I look behind the veil; I see a reflection of myself.

Why don't we go beyond the broken-down wall? Sometimes it means we have to leave our own comfort zones. On June 7 of 1996, I turned the television on in Louisville, Kentucky, and saw a white pastor being interviewed by a news reporter. He was asked, "Why did you not allow this little black boy who was invited by his little white friend, a member of your church, to worship in your church?" The pastor said, "I am the pastor of this church, and I decide who can and who cannot come into this building." To go beyond the broken-down wall means we must leave our comfort zone.

I know a church that had a ministry to Hispanic migrant workers, and they provided for them at a distance, but when the request was made for the Hispanic migrants to be permitted to worship in their sanctuary, the word came back to the person who was ministering to them, "We don't want those Mexicans in our building."

Brothers and sisters, if we are to go beyond the wall, it means we must leave our comfort zone; it means that we must share power. We don't mind sitting at the table with one another as long as we don't share power. Unfortunately, around our tables there are those who have power but have no conscience, and there are those who have conscience but have no power. We need people who sit around the table with both power and conscience who are not after self-aggrandizement but who are after the advancement of the kingdom of God.

To move beyond the veil in essence means that I've got to do something about where I am: for seeing is not just believing, seeing is relieving. That's what Jesus said in Matthew 25:35–40: The imprisoned are visited; the naked are clothed; the hungry are fed. He was the exemplar, for he taught those who were unlearned; he touched the lepers; he ate with sinners; he associated with publicans; he took the outcasts and made them a part of his family. If we are to go beyond the wall, we must relieve or minister to what we see. But it will take more than just seeing, and it will take more than just talking.

God had been talking for a long time, talking through forty-two generations, talking through prophets, talking through priests, talking through kings, but it was not enough. He had been talking through John the Baptist, the precursor of Jesus, but it was not enough. Jesus had been talking, but it was not enough—talking from boats, talking in the temple, talking from hillsides, but it was not enough. He had been talking when he used the Beatitudes as a way of propagating truth, talking through parables, giving the Olivet Discourse, but they were not enough. It was only on the cross of Calvary when he acted and died that the veil in the temple was rent from top to bottom and the middle wall of partition was broken down.

It is time for us to see; it is time for us to move; but it is also time for us to act. May we affirm with all that is within us the truth of this hymn:

A charge to keep I have, a God to glorify,
A never dying soul to save and fit it for the sky.
Arm me with jealous care as in thy sight to live,
And oh, thy servant Lord prepare a strict account to give.
To serve this present age, my calling to fulfill;
Oh, may it all my power engage to do my Master's will.

Chapter 12

The Sin of Inhospitality

TIMOTHY GEORGE
Luke 9:46–62

When Jesus came to earth to fulfill the mission his Father had given him to do, what strategy did he use to carry out that awesome task? Jesus never wrote a book. As far as we know, he never wrote anything except a few letters in the sand. Jesus did not found an institution, not even a theological seminary. He never held a huge evangelistic crusade. What did Jesus do? What was his strat-egy? He chose twelve men, and he said, "You guys, come follow me. Wherever I go, you go. What I do, you will see." Through those twelve disciples, he instituted a plan to change the whole world. They learned much from his parables, his miracles, and his deeds. But the greatest lessons were often the en-counters that happened as they walked with him along the roads of Galilee.

TIMOTHY GEORGE *is the founding dean of Beeson Divinity School at Samford University, and senior editor of* Christianity Today. *He holds degrees from the University of Tennessee at Chattanooga (B.A.), Harvard Divinity School (M.Div.) and Harvard University (Th.D.). A noted historian and theologian, he has written and edited numerous books, including* Theology of the Reformers, Baptist Theologians, John Calvin and the Church, Faithful Witness: The Life and Mission of William Carey, *and the volume on Galatians in the* New American Commentary. *He is a member of the Doctrine Commission of the Baptist World Alliance and serves on the boards of Prison Fellowship Ministries, the Center for Catholic and Evangelical Theology, and Wheaton College.*

In Luke 9, we have three incidents that happened in the life of Jesus as the disciples were walking with him along the way. Each of these events was a teaching moment for them and for us. We see here three great roadblocks on the way to reconciliation, each of them related to the primal sin of inhospitality.

"An argument started among the disciples as to which of them would be the greatest" (Luke 9:46 NIV). Jesus' disciples have been fussing for a long time! Controversy is nothing new. It goes all the way back to this band of disciples, walking along beside Jesus, who began to argue and fight among themselves. They were not fighting here with the Pharisees. They were not fighting with the Sadducees. Nor were they fighting with the Zealots, the Essenes, or some other esoteric group. They were fighting among themselves.

And what were they fighting about? Surely it must have been about something very important, perhaps the doctrine of the Holy Trinity? How can the Father and the Son and the Holy Spirit be three distinct persons and yet one God? Was that the problem that vexed those disciples? Or maybe it was a deep christological paradox. How can the God-man be both entirely divine and yet at the same time fully human, the hypostatic union of the Son of God? If not that, perhaps it was ecclesiology? Do we have open communion or closed communion? That's worth fighting about. Surely it was something like that! An argument started among the disciples, and what were they fighting about? "As to which of them would be the greatest."

Who is the greatest? On another occasion, James and John came to Jesus and said, "Lord, when you come into your kingdom, which one of us will be on your right hand and which on your left? Who's number one and who's number two in the new administration? You let us know." Right in the middle of that little word *sin* is the letter "I." "I will ascend above the stars of God. I will be seated on the throne of God." Who first said that?

The devil. And now the disciples of Jesus were echoing not the voice of their Father in heaven, but the siren of the fiend of hell. The Bible says, "Jesus, knowing their thoughts" (Luke 9:47 NIV). You can't hide anything from him. He is a mind-reading Savior. Jesus knew what they were thinking. Now he may not have heard all of their arguments. They were over there in the groves fighting among themselves, but Jesus with radar sensitivity pierced right through the exterior into their hearts. In response to this childish bickering, Jesus took a real child, and had that little child stand beside him: a living object lesson, a human being, a little child.

In Jesus' world, as in ours, children lived on the margins of society. They were nobodies. They were among the most vulnerable, least protected, least cared-about members of ancient society. It is the same in our world today—among children, both born and unborn. It is ironic, I think, that some of those who are most concerned about abortion have little to say about race relations. And some of those most concerned about racism have very little to say about abortion. But the two are vitally connected because they have to do with the value that God Almighty puts on a human life.

Jesus took a little child and put the child beside these bickering, selfish, narcissistic disciples. Jesus was concerned about those who were on the margins of society. Do you know the people who really roam through the Gospel of Luke? What's Luke about? Luke talks a lot about women. Only in Luke do we learn about Elizabeth and Mary and the birth of Jesus and all those things that went on. Luke is the one who tells us about shepherds. We have romanticized the shepherds in our Christmas pageants. We bring them in and doll them up, and they are so sweet-smelling and clean, like little angels right from heaven. But shepherds were people who stank. They had a dirty job. They were at the lowest level of society. And the lepers. So many lepers. Unclean! Jesus touched them, embraced them, loved them, healed them. Tax collectors, Samaritans—those are the kinds of people that Jesus was concerned about, and among them was this little child.

In the nineteenth century there was a little girl in Chicago, Illinois, who used to walk all the way across Chicago to attend the church where D. L. Moody was pastor. She had to walk by a lot of churches to get from where she lived over to where that church was. Someone asked her one time, "Little girl, why do you walk by all these churches to go all the way across town every Sunday to Mr. Moody's church?" She said, "Over there at Mr. Moody's church, they love little girls like me."

"Whoever welcomes this little child in my name welcomes me; and whoever welcomes me welcomes the one who sent me" (Luke 9:48 NIV). Did you notice this word *welcome?* The greatest sin against the Lord Jesus Christ was the sin of inhospitality. They didn't welcome him. There was no room for him in the inn. There was no room for him in Nazareth either. They ran him out of town. Finally, there was no room for him in Jerusalem, and they nailed him on a cross. He came unto his own and his own received him not. This is the sin of inhospitality.

But notice, too, how Jesus identified himself with this little child. "If you welcome me, you will welcome this one." There is a connection, an identification there. And the opposite is also true: if you don't welcome this little one, then you won't welcome me. Jesus spells it out in another passage in the New Testament when he's talking about the last judgment. On that great day, everybody's going to come there and they will say, "Lord, we did a lot of things in your name. We cast out demons, and we had great Sunday school conferences, and we published a lot of literature, and we did many wonderful things." And Jesus will essentially say, "I was in prison and I never saw you come to see me. I was down there in the gutter and you never helped me out, and as much as you have done it unto the least of these, you've done it unto me" (Matt. 25:34–40).

Recently I met a fine young pastor who invited all the children in the community to come to Vacation Bible School at his church. They put a big sign out front, "Everybody welcome!" Vacation Bible School, Kool-Aid, and cookies—that won't hurt anybody. He invited them to come, and some of them came. One of the little girls, an African-American girl, was placed in the Vacation Bible School class of the matriarch of that church. The pastor said she came to his office with the little girl and said, "Preacher, you invited her. Now you can teach her!" If you do it to the least of these, you do it to me.

Last Easter Sunday, I preached from Luke 16:19–31, the story of the rich man and Lazarus. The rich man in hell is talking to Father Abraham and he says, "Father Abraham, I wish you would send somebody to warn my brothers so they won't come to this horrible place." Father Abraham says, "Well, they have Moses and the prophets. Even if somebody rose from the dead, they wouldn't believe it." (That's why this is a proper Easter text: somebody did rise from the dead, and they still don't believe it!) What was the sin of that rich man in hell? Inhospitality. He had a beggar at his gate, and he wouldn't pass the bread. It wasn't his bread. "The earth is the LORD's and the fulness thereof" (Ps. 24:1). God gave him a good chunk of bread, but he wouldn't pass the bread. Crumbs fell from his table, and he ended up in hell because of the sin of inhospitality.

Isn't it interesting how eating together is such a sensitive thing? The Civil Rights Movement—when it really got started, it was about lunch counters, wasn't it? Eating together. Jesus was OK as long as he was doing miracles and even teaching the Sermon on the Mount. They could stand that. But when he began to eat with those kinds of people: "This man receiveth sinners, and eateth with them," they said (Luke 15:2). That was too much.

So Jesus turned their world upside down: he proclaimed an inversion of values. He said, "For he who is least among you all—he is the greatest" (Luke 9:48 NIV). Who is the greatest? "He who is least." "As you did it to one of the least of these" (Matt. 25:40 NKJV). In the ministry of Jesus there is this marvelous turn-about, this reversal, where outsiders become insiders. A Roman centurion, an enemy soldier, exclaimed, "Lord . . . just say the word, and my servant will be healed" (Matt. 8:8 NIV). And Jesus said, "I haven't seen faith like this in all the land of Israel!" (Matt. 8:10 NLT). A Roman soldier!

Or he's having dinner at Simon the Pharisees's house and all the big shots in town are there, and this prostitute comes in, this woman from the gutter. She begins to weep and to anoint the feet of Jesus with her tears and to kiss his feet. Everybody is shocked, but Jesus says, "Her sins, which are many, are forgiven, for she loved much" (Luke 7:47 NKJV). Or that banquet. Jesus said a man gave a banquet and nobody came; everybody was too busy. They had all these excuses. And then he said, "You go out into the highways and the hedges and bring in the lame, and the poor and the blind, these nobodies on the margins of society, the least of these, and you tell them, 'Come to dinner. Everything's ready for you'" (Luke 14:16–24). No wonder they call it "amazing" grace!

Inhospitality is closely related to a second obstacle on the road to reconciliation: the sin of insularity. *Insul* is the Latin word for island, and insularity is to cut yourself off from everybody else into a little self-contained island, floating alone in the ocean of humanity. "'Master,' said John, 'we saw a man driving out demons in your name and we tried to stop him, because he is not one of us.' 'Do not stop him,' Jesus said, 'for whoever is not against you is for you'" (Luke 9:49–50 NIV).

Jesus is not giving here a stamp of approval for the kind of open-ended, easy-going ecumenism that results in a bland togetherness at the expense of theological integrity. In fact, just a few verses later, in Luke 11:23, Jesus seems to say the exact opposite of what he said to the disciples earlier: "He who is not with me is against me, and he who does not gather with me, scatters" (NIV). Jesus does not agree with those who say that it doesn't matter what you believe, just as long as you're nice. What you believe does matter, and it matters eternally.

Jesus was dealing with a different problem in Luke 9. Here was an exorcist, a man who was driving out demons, and he was doing it in Jesus' name. But the disciples of Jesus got real huffy. They tried to stop him. Perhaps they tore down his evangelistic posters, or maybe they began to gossip behind his back and say, "You don't want to go to that guy." I don't know what they did, but somehow they tried to stop his ministry.

And why did they do this? Could it have been jealousy? Earlier in the Gospel of Luke, we read about a person who was filled with demons and was brought to the disciples for help, but they were not able to do a thing about it. They could not even cast out one puny demon. And now this freelancer, this guy who doesn't have a degree, is not properly ordained, is out doing what Jesus' own disciples could not do. And they tried to stop him. Why? Not because his theology was heretical, nor his life immoral, but simply because he was not "one of us."

The sin of racism is not unrelated to the fact of sectarianism. Both are blights on the church of Jesus Christ. Many Christians today draw the line of fellowship in the same insular way as the disciples of Jesus in this text. We reject other believers simply because "they're not one of us." We ostracize one another on the basis of this invidious principle: "If you don't hate my enemy as much as I hate my enemy, then you just can't be my friend!" How will we ever be able to reach out across racial lines when we are so divided internally among ourselves? God is calling on us to repent of the sin of insularity.

In this catena of events Luke has brought together, inhospitality and insularity lead inevitably to a third great stumbling block on the road to reconciliation: the sin of inhumanity. Jesus was going to Jerusalem and he sent messengers on ahead. They went into a Samaritan village to get things ready for him, but the people did not welcome them. When James and John, the thunderstorm boys, saw this, they said, "Lord, do you want us to call fire down from heaven to destroy them?" (Luke 9:54 NIV).

This event confronts us with the kind of mutual suspicion and recrimination that takes root in our lives when prejudice reigns. This was a Samaritan village. Half-breeds, a people of mixed race—they were part Jew and part Gentile. They had been living in Samaria for hundreds of years. They had developed their own temple and their own culture. They even had their own version of the Pentateuch, the Samaritan Pentateuch. They had their own way of doing things; they were segregated from the rest of the country, and they were despised by the Jews. And they felt the same way about the Jews too. The hostility was mutual.

What is prejudice? Prejudice literally means to judge in advance. It means not to deal with a person as a person, but to put on that person all kinds of stereotypes. All Jews are stingy. All blacks are lazy. All whites are racists. All men are chauvinists. All women are devious. All fundamentalists are ignorant. That is prejudice.

How quickly prejudice can erupt into violence. "Let's call fire down from heaven and burn 'em to a crisp! Just say the word, and we'll nuke 'em!" Where does fighting and violence come from? James asks that question and he gives the answer: It comes from inside your heart. It comes from not being right with God (James 4:1–3).

Remember these were the disciples of Jesus. The man who wrote the Gospel of John about love and all that stuff. But here he wanted to call fire down from heaven and wipe these people off the face of the earth. They didn't go into Samaria to start a race war. They didn't go into Samaria to cause rioting in the streets. They went there to preach the gospel, to save souls. This was an evangelistic campaign. But somewhere along the way, something went wrong. And so Jesus had to step in and say to them, "Boys, we are not going to do it that way! Let's go on to another town."

Jesus did not give up on Samaria. Remember John 4, the woman at the well? Through Jesus' loving encounter with that outcast woman, an entire Samaritan village—it might have been this same town as far as we know—received the living water of eternal life. But here in Luke 9, Jesus rebuked the sin of inhumanity among his own disciples.

Jesus was teaching the disciples an important lesson that we also need desperately to learn: If you're going to come out where God comes out, you have to take God's way to get there. Do you see the progression here? You start with the inhospitality, which leads to insularity—"you are not one of us"—and, before long, you've descended to inhumanity. Three steps down into the pit. And we must all be careful lest we slide unknowingly toward this infernal destination.

For it is not just "them" out there, *those* racists, *those* Kluxers, *those* extremists. It's also "us" in here. If we are going to follow Jesus, then the devotion we have for him must be reflected in our attitude toward others, for all the others have been created in the image of God, and they are precious in his sight.

Chapter 13

We're All in This Together

FRED LUTER JR.
1 Corinthians 12:12–27

If I were to take an informal poll about America's greatest need, I'm sure I would get a wide range of responses. I'm sure most of us would agree that we're living in some perilous times. I'm sure most of us would agree that we're living in a sin-sick society. And it appears that things are not getting any better.

So the questions are asked—"What would get America on the right track? What is the antidote that would heal our diseased nation? Just what is the greatest need of our country?"

Well, in this informal poll, I'm sure one group would say that America's greatest need is "economic reform." We need to create more jobs. We need to stop the downsizing of companies. We need to stop the layoffs.

FRED LUTER JR. *is pastor of Franklin Avenue Baptist Church in New Orleans. Dr. Luter has studied at the University of New Orleans, New Orleans Baptist Theological Seminary, and Lake Charles Bible College (D.Min.). Since Dr. Luter became pastor of Franklin Avenue Baptist Church in 1986, this congregation has grown from sixty-five to a participating membership of more than three thousand. Dr. Luter has served on the executive board of the Louisiana Baptist Convention and, in 1996, was elected as 2nd vice president of the Southern Baptist Convention. He also serves as a trustee of LifeWay Christian Resources of the Southern Baptist Convention. In this sermon, "We're All in This Together," Dr. Luter describes something of his own personal experience both of the pain of persistent racism and the joy of victory over prejudice and discrimination.*

We need equal opportunities for everyone. That would get us on the right track—economic reform. But then I would hurriedly disagree with that group. Yes, economic reform is important and it has its place, but economic reform is *not* America's greatest need.

Then another group would say that America's greatest need is health care. There are a growing number of senior citizens who require some type of medical care, with our elderly needing assistance from Medicare and/or Medicaid. There are an even greater number of individuals who can't afford to get sick because of the high cost of medical services. Because of the number of hospitals that will turn you away at the emergency room door because there is no insurance, oh yes, health care is our greatest need. But then again, I would hurriedly disagree with that group. Yes, health care is important and it has its place, but health care is *not* America's greatest need.

By then another group would speak up, claiming that America's greatest need is to deal with our drug abuse problem. And who would deny that we need to stop the drug flow in America—it's everywhere! It's in major cities as well as small towns. It's in the suburbs as well as the inner city. It's in the White House as well as in the schoolhouse. It's being used by the rich as well as the poor. It's being used by the young as well as the old. It's being used by the yuppies as well as the buppies. Oh yes, if we could get a handle on the drug problem in America, that would get us on the right track. Yet again, I would hurriedly disagree with that group. Yes, dealing with the illegal drug problem is important and it has its place, but drug abuse is *not* America's greatest need.

At that time, another group would speak up to say crime is our greatest problem. No, says another, education is crucial. AIDS and other sexually transmitted diseases is America's greatest need, shouts another group. And again I would object to each statement. Now, don't get me wrong; all of these issues are crucial. All are legitimate concerns. All are important subjects that must be addressed. But at the root of all these ailments is an even greater sickness!

America's main problem is that we are suffering from a severe case of spiritual malnutrition. And the only remedy, the only antidote, is for the church to stand up and be the church!

God's people must stand up and be the church! We must accept the mandate that God has given to us in Matthew 28:19–20, "Go ye therefore, and teach all nations, baptizing them in the name of the Father, and of the Son, and of the Holy Ghost: Teaching them to observe all things whatsoever I have commanded you: and, lo, I am with you alway, even unto the end of the world. Amen." Oh my friends, those are our marching orders; that's our mandate; that's our mission. America will live or die depending on the role that we play as the church. And if the church is to be effective in carrying out our mission, we must realize that "we're all in this together." We must, as the body of Christ, come together as one!

You see, my friend, one of Satan's most effective strategies is to convince us that we are competing against each other. He pits one group against another: Baptist against Methodist; Southern Baptist against National Baptist; National Baptist against Full Gospel Baptist; preacher against preacher; ministry against ministry; and church against church. Think about it. In many cities in America there are churches on almost every corner. All those churches on all those corners, all those sermons, all those choirs, and all those ministries—yet our cities are in a constant state of darkness because of sin. Oh, my brothers and sisters, there's something wrong with that picture. And what's wrong is that the church is not coming together as the church. Satan has been quite successful at separating us from one another: the large churches from the small churches; the inner city from the suburbs; the haves from the have-nots, and the list goes on.

But I believe the most serious and most effective attack against the church is in the area of racism. There is too much separation in our churches between races and cultures. More than any other wall that separates the church, I believe this wall has been the most effective. This wall that separates blacks, whites, Hispanics, Asians, Koreans or any other group must come down if we're truly going to be the church that God has called us to be!

Listen, my friend, I'm convinced we can change our cities. I'm convinced we can change our states. I'm convinced we can change our country. But we first must tear down the racial walls that divide us. We first must tear down the racial barriers that separate us. If there is any hope for America, the church must come together as one body. We are different races, different cultures, and different backgrounds, but we are one body coming together. Toe to toe, ankle to ankle, knee to knee, waist to waist, chest to chest, and shoulder to shoulder, we are all members of one body. That's what Paul is addressing in our text as he writes to the Corinthian church.

Now here was a church that had it going on! This Corinthian church did not lack anything. They had talented leaders. They had dedicated members. They had spiritual gifts. They had a great name. They had the potential to be a great church. However, there was one major problem in this church—the members of the body couldn't get along! So here in our text, the founding pastor of this Corinthian church tries to resolve the problems in this membership by reminding them that we're *all* members of Christ's body. In other words, we're all in this together.

There are three things I want us to see in this text.

First, we're all one father's children (1 Cor. 12:12–13). Listen my friend, if you've been born again; if you've accepted Jesus Christ into your life as Lord and Savior; if you've been saved by his blood; if you've been raised by his power; if you know and believe that Jesus was born of a virgin, lived a sinless life, died on Calvary for the sins of the world, rose again from the grave with all power, and is one day coming back again for his bride, the church, so that we may live eternally with him, well, my friend, if you believe all of this, then it doesn't matter what your skin color; it doesn't matter your race; it doesn't matter your cultural background.

The fact of the matter is, if God is your Father, you are my brother and my sister! In other words, "we're all one Father's children"! That's what Paul was trying to say to the Corinthian church. Whether we're Jews or Gentiles, whether we are bond or free, we're all one Father's children. We are many members, many shades, many colors, many lives, but all belonging to the same Father.

My father and mother were divorced when I was a child about six years old. Both of them eventually remarried. My dad had two other children from his second marriage. However, one of the blessings that came out of that situation is that we have never referred to each other as "step" brother or "half" sister. By the grace of God, we have always referred to each other as brothers and sisters. I believe God wants the same thing to happen in the body of Christ. If we are born-again believers, then God is the Father of all of us! Red, yellow, black, and white, we're all precious in his sight.

God has opened a lot of doors for me in my ministry. One of the areas where God has really proved himself has been in the area of racial reconciliation. I have been used by God to tear down a lot of walls that have been built up over the years, particularly in our local, state, and national convention. God has opened doors to me that were not available before, resulting in my becoming the first African American in some of these roles and positions: The first African American as a trustee in our local association; the first African American elected as a vice-president of our state convention; the first African American to serve as a trustee in one of our national agencies; and the one I'm most proud of—the first African American to speak in the pulpits of many of the white churches in Louisiana.

I'm most proud of the latter accomplishment because it has been during those times of standing in a strange pulpit, in front of a strange crowd that I've seen God literally tear down the walls of racial prejudice. One of the most touching moments when I saw the hand of God move was on the last night of a revival service. It was the first time this church had ever had an African-American preacher in the pulpit. During that revival I stood each night and preached from the Word of God. I preached the birth, life, death, burial, and resurrection of our Lord and Savior Jesus Christ! I preached about sin, faith, salvation, and the joy of knowing Christ. God moved in a mighty way that week, but he saved the best for the last night.

As the pastor of the church was giving his closing announcements and thanking the choir, congregation, and guests for supporting the revival, an elderly member stood up and said, "Pastor, there is something I must say." I could not help but notice the pastor bow his head and say, "Oh, my Lord." About that same time many in the congregation began making facial expressions and whispering to each other. Something was about to happen here, and nobody knew what to expect.

The congregation grew silent as the elderly man began to say: "Pastor, y'all know I was not in agreement with bringing this *colored* preacher to our church." Immediately, you could hear the groans and moans throughout the membership as this man ended his sentence. I looked at the pastor and his head was still bowed, and then I looked for the nearest door because I was about to get out of Dodge!

Then this man said something that shocked everyone. He spoke as tears began to roll down his face, "But after hearing this young man preach; after hearing him share the gospel; after hearing him share his heart, I stand before God and this congregation asking that you would forgive me of my ignorance." You talk about a shout in the camp! Oh, it happened that night. I wish those of you who are reading this sermon could have seen God move as that elderly man after the service, in the presence of his pastor, his family, and members of the church approached me, embraced me, asked me to forgive him—and loud enough so everyone nearby could hear—said, "I love you, my brother." Oh, in the words of an old Baptist preacher, "Ain't God good!" We're all one Father's children.

The second thing I want you to see in this text is that we're all members of the same body. "For the body is not one member but many. If the foot shall say, Because I am not the hand, I am not of the body; is it therefore not of the body? And if the ear shall say, Because I am not the eye, I am not of the body; is it therefore not of the body? If the whole body were an eye, where were the hearing? If the whole were hearing, where were the smelling? But now hath God set the members every one of them in the body, as it hath pleased him" (1 Cor. 12:14–18). Oh, the church at Corinth was a messed-up church. Instead of depending on each other; instead of being who God made them, they constantly complained about one another. Each of them were assuming that because they were not fulfilling a certain function, they were not of the body.

And, my brothers and sisters, this is another area where the enemy has been able to separate us. Listen, there are and will be differences among us, but we must realize that we're all members of the same body. The music in the Anglo church may be different from the music in the African-American church. The music in the Baptist church may be different from the music in the Asian church. The style of black preachers is different from that of white preachers. Asian sermons may be different from Hispanic sermons. Ministries in inner-city churches may be different from ministries in the suburbs, but the fact is that we are all members of the same body.

As I heard my mentor, Dr. Tony Evans of Oak Cliff Bible Fellowship in Dallas, Texas, say, "God does not expect white folk to like R & B music and he sho-nuff does not expect blacks to like country and western music!" We all don't have the same functions, we all don't minister the same way, but we must all accept each other as members of the same body.

When I do a pulpit exchange with one of my Anglo brothers, I don't expect him to preach like a black preacher at Franklin Avenue because the congregation is predominantly black. I want him to be who he is. If he's an eye, don't act like an ear. If he's a foot, don't act like a head. He needs to be himself. Because when I stand in his pulpit before a predominantly white congregation, I'm not going to change my preaching style. I'm going to be who God has called me to be.

Yes, our skin color is different. Yes, our culture is different. Yes, our background may be different. Yes, our style of worship may be different, but the moment we said yes to the Lord, we became members of the same body—the body of Christ! Therefore, white Christians can't say to black Christians, "I don't need you." Nor can Hispanic Christians say to Asian Christians, "I don't need you." Because we're all members of the same body, we need one another.

And this leads to my third and final point: we're all in this together (vv. 22–27). Paul says in verse 24 that God put the body together. In verse 25 he says that there should be no division in the body, but that the members should have the same care for one another. If this Corinthian church had understood how crucial it was for them to work together, they never would have gone through the arguments and disagreements that kept affecting their church. Because of their selfishness, their carnality, their lack of commitment, and their disobedience to God, they never experienced the joy and blessings of working together as one body.

Cannot this be said about the church today? Satan has done a good job of separating us by classes, denominations, and particularly by race. It is hard to believe that 11:00 A.M. on Sunday morning is still the most segregated time in America. It is a sad fact that there are still some churches in which you are not welcome because of the color of your skin. About three years ago, a pastor in north Louisiana called to cancel a revival that he had invited me to preach because the deacons found out I was black. I also can remember a white pastor who wanted to deal with racial reconciliation at his church by having me preach there. Because it was a church that had a history of racism, he was afraid to invite me.

I told him jokingly, "Tell them I pastor a leading church in the convention. Tell them the various positions I hold in the convention. Tell them whatever you need to tell them; just don't put my picture on the publicity flyers!" The only reason I was not welcome in that pulpit was because of the color of my skin. When will we realize that we're all in this together?

Think about what could happen in America if the racial walls would come down. What if churches of different races came together for the cause of Christ? What if the doors of every church in America were open to anybody and everybody, regardless of race or color of skin? What do you think would happen in our cities, in our states, and in our nation if the walls of racism came down? Well, I'll tell you what would happen. God would send a revival in this land! We would be able to reclaim, from the devil, all that he has stolen from the children of God.

Remember, the Bible says that if God's people, all of God's people, every color, creed, and culture "will humble themselves and pray and seek [God's] face and turn from their wicked ways, then will [he] hear from heaven and will forgive their sin and will heal their land" (2 Chron. 7:14 NIV). In other words there will be a revival in the land!

If America needs anything today, we need a revival!

• Economic reform is valid—but we need a revival!

• Health care is essential—but we need a revival!

• Drug abuse must be addressed—but we need a revival!

• Crime has to cease—but we need a revival!

• Education is crucial—but we need a revival!

• Finding a cure for AIDS and other sexually transmitted diseases is important—but we need a revival!

• And in order for America to experience a revival, the churches across the nation must realize that we're all one Father's children; we're all members of the same body, and we're all in this together. In the words of a song my grandmother used to sing, "Get right church—and let's go home!"

Chapter 14

The Way to Peace and Harmony

Luder G. Whitlock Jr.

Ephesians 2:14–22

Long ago and far away peace and harmony ruled in a place called paradise. It might have stayed that way too, except for a fateful decision about food. It happened when Adam and Eve disobeyed God and ate the one fruit he had specifically told them not to eat (Gen. 2:15–17). It may have seemed to be a trivial decision at the moment, perhaps one with promise of rising to a new level of knowledge like that of God, but the results were cataclysmic—the very opposite of what they expected (Gen. 3:4–7).

This disobedient act shattered the idyllic harmony of paradise, resulting in the immediate destruction of their

Luder G. Whitlock Jr. is president of Reformed Theological Seminary. He holds degrees from the University of Florida (B.A.), Westminster Theological Seminary (M.Div.), and Vanderbilt University (D.Min.). Dr. Whitlock serves on numerous boards, including the National Commission on Higher Education, the National Association of Evangelicals, and the Mission America National Committee. He is also president of the Association of Theological Schools in the United States and Canada. He has edited and contributed to many scholarly projects, including The New Geneva Study Bible, The Evangelical Dictionary of Theology, Reformed Theology in America, and The Dictionary of Twentieth Century Christian Biography.

Dr. Whitlock brings a spirit of healing and reconciliation to his many leadership roles in both the academy and the church. In this sermon, "The Way to Peace and Harmony," he calls the Christian community to follow the path of reconciling love and forgiveness set forth in the redeeming mission of Jesus Christ.

relationship with God and their relationship with each other and the created world, including the animals. The estrangement, tension, and hostility that followed were new experiences. Stunned and ashamed, they hid from God, then turned on each other. Too late, after they were banished from their idyllic setting, they began to realize what they had lost.

Soon the consequences of their sin became all too evident when their son Cain murdered his brother Abel in cold blood (Gen. 4:8). It was a tragic moment in early human history when brother turned violently against brother. Looking back through the lens of Scripture, we now realize that alienation, estrangement, loneliness, and the various other forms of flawed and broken relationships that infect our lives find their origin in that first sin of Adam and Eve. Little did they realize what pain and misery they would inflict on all who came after them.

The rest of the Bible offers an unfolding commentary about the damage to human relationships resulting from their sin. The story of the tower of Babel is a pertinent illustration. It was probably a ziggurat, with small steps up for people and big ones down for the deity. It was a vain attempt to reach up to God and bring him down among the people through human effort, but the tower further compounded human estrangement from God and from one another. When God came, he unexpectedly came in judgment, with terrible consequences (Gen. 11:1–9).

The movie *The Bible* captured it well by showing how friends and neighbors who were working together side by side on this great tower suddenly lost the ability to communicate with one another. They were abruptly speaking different languages and could not understand one another. Frustration at being unable to communicate shifted quickly to suspicion and enmity. Fearfully they ran away, seeking safety and protection. Since that time communication and community have been elusive, with the result that human relationships have too often led to disillusionment and hurt. Think of Joseph and his brothers, David and Bathsheba, or the disciples of Jesus and the Pharisees.

Why do people have trouble getting along? Why do they quarrel and fight? Why is human history strewn with the wreckage of war and stained with bloodshed? Why have racial groups hated and been hated? Why is there so much hurtful hostility? After thinking about all the pain and trauma in human experience, it is easy to understand why it's been said, "The more I see of people, the more I like my dog." What a price has been paid for biting into that forbidden fruit—the tragic disobedience of Adam and Eve. The real tragedy is that everyone suffers. But deep down, people don't want this kind of trouble that makes life ugly and painful.

To the contrary, there is an endemic desire to be loved and understood because at the core of our identity we are relational. We were created for companionship, made for the sharing of love and life, and we are restless and incomplete without it (Gen. 2:18, 21–24). As John Donne put it, "No man is an island." There is no way we can exist completely independent and separate from others. From our births that tie us to our parents, in one way or another we discover our attachment to and our need for others. So we yearn for genuine, satisfying relationships, not tension and hostility. But sin distorts and warps our inner longings.

Sometimes this happens in unusual ways, such as homosexuality: the attraction of one male to another or one female to another. Yet homosexuality must be seen as a perversion of the normal desire for love and companionship. As such it reflects God's judgment against sin, forcefully noted by Paul in Romans 1:26–32. Who would have expected that at the close of the twentieth century the gay life would be condoned and openly promoted? What is even more shocking is the acceptance of homosexuality by some sectors of American Christianity, sanctioning gay marriages and endorsing the ordination of homosexuals. This is no isolated problem, but rather a reflection of contemporary reality. As such it underscores the distortion of our inner longings that can be caused by sin.

There are many other forms of the damage sin has done to relationships. If anything, our modern era of huge cities and dazzling technology has resulted in a rapid disintegration of society. Strange isn't it, that you can "reach out and touch someone" by phone or E-mail via the Internet, yet it is more difficult than ever to connect personally, and relationships seem more fragile than ever. Family solidarity has evaporated, replaced by fragile ties and more and more frequently by dysfunctionality. No wonder it has been said we are a nation of strangers. Cities breed anonymity as people get lost in the masses. Crime grows like a weed fertilized by that anonymity. Its fruit is a new form of hostility—like the "road rage" that leads to violent acts among commuting traffic or the anger that erupts into a shooting spree in a factory or fast-food franchise.

In spite of our efforts to build a democracy where all people are treated equally with liberty and justice for all, seldom has the ideal prevailed. Native Americans have often been exploited and oppressed. Years ago when the West was being won, "the only good Indian is a dead Indian" marked the attitudes of too many immigrant Americans. The experience of Native Americans at the hands of the new Americans is an embarrassment, but it is not unique. Similar prejudicial attitudes prevailed against other ethnic groups, such as Mexicans and Asians.

Racial hostility has left deep, lasting scars on our ethnic mosaic, marking a breach between blacks and whites that stubbornly persists. Tied to slavery, reconstruction and segregation, feelings remain strong, sometimes smoldering, sometimes erupting into flames, as with the rioting and violence in Los Angeles following the Rodney King incident.

Notorious incidents such as the brutal murder of James Byrd Jr. in Texas—who was beaten, then chained to a pick-up truck and dragged several miles along a road until his head and right arm were severed—are grisly reminders that the problem of racism continues. This rupture is especially troubling to Christians, who know it does not fit Christianity because in Christ all the distinctions that separate are removed. He tears down the walls that divide, reconciling us to God and to one another (Eph. 2:14–22).

So whenever relationships take a nasty turn, it is especially troubling to believers who realize that it is incongruous with true Christianity. The Scriptures make it plain that through his atoning death on the cross Christ removed the barriers that divide us from one another as well as from God. He was rejected and despised. He was ridiculed and scorned, imprisoned and beaten. He was taken outside the city walls, then was crucified. But, remember, when he died, abandoned and God-forsaken, he made sure we never would be abandoned, rejected, or forsaken by God. Rather, through repentance and faith in him we would be accepted by the Father. Now, reconciled to him by faith, we join the beloved circle of those whose names are written in the Book of Life.

In Ephesians 2:11 and following, Paul explains how this has happened, emphasizing that Christ "has destroyed the barrier, the dividing wall of hostility" (v. 14 NIV). His purpose was to reconcile the Jew and the Gentile foreigner to God through the cross, making peace between them so that they "are no longer foreigners and aliens, but fellow citizens with God's people and members of God's household" (v. 19 NIV). The mystery of the gospel is the wonder of God's reconciling love that brings former enemies—Jews and Gentiles—together as members of one family who love each other and share life together as children of their Father in heaven (Eph. 3:3–6).

There are so many things that can divide: education, social status, culture, race, and experience. The list continues because it is easy to tear down but hard to build. What has been undone or broken can be extremely difficult to mend. The beauty of the gospel is that in Christ we are joined together into one new family. We belong! We retain our diversity, of course, but through the Holy Spirit's influence the things that would normally divide us become instrumental in fusing us into a new unity as our various gifts are harnessed into one harmonious effort. Through the gospel, God destroys our divisions and enmity, reconciling us to himself and to each other.

So when we speak of salvation, redemption, or eternal life, we cannot afford to ignore the word *reconciliation.* In 2 Corinthians, Paul describes God's great work of reconciliation, accomplished by the sinless Son of God who took our sin on himself so that we might become the righteousness of God in him (5:21). God was reconciling the world to himself in Christ, Paul says, not counting our sins against us but finding a way to forgive us and to reconcile us to himself. So the first great effect of salvation is reconciliation to God and the immediate discovery of fellowship with him, the recovery of the relationship that was lost through that first sin of Adam and Eve (Rom. 5:12–21).

The second discovery is that because we are new creatures in Christ, we are no longer able to regard others "from a worldly point of view" (2 Cor. 5:16 NIV). Therefore, we develop a passion for reconciling others to God so they may share our experience. Then we develop a passion for reconciling ourselves to others, for in Christ there is no longer Jew or Gentile, male or female. Since we are all one through faith in Christ and are part of his family (Gal. 3:28–29), we experience an innate desire to express that by reaching out to others.

One test of our new status before God—the reality of our reconciliation—is genuine effort to obey him. We demonstrate our love for him and our desire to make him smile when our utmost effort is expended to please him. Similarly, we also demonstrate this new spiritual status by extending true love to others. The Lord's children must acknowledge his call, not only to be at peace with him, but with one another. This is especially for those who are estranged and hostile, knowing that in doing so we demonstrate our new identity. After all, it's easy to love those who love you; problem people are the challenge (Matt. 5:43–48). God is displeased when we erect walls to divide us from one another. The degree to which we create division demonstrates a substantial spiritual deficiency.

The apostle John, attempting to help believers ascertain the authenticity of their faith with a measure of certainty, offered three tests. One is love for one another. John persistently pursues this point, culminating with his assertion that "whoever does not love does not know God, because God is love" (1 John 4:8 NIV). He continues his argument by observing that if you say you love God but do not love your brother, then there is an inconsistency, if not a contradiction. If you don't love your brother whom you see all the time, he asks, how can you love God when you have never even seen him? (v. 20). His point is clear.

Authentic Christianity heals our relationship with God and our human relationships. Francis Schaeffer said it well in *True Spirituality* and his well-known *Two Contents, Two Realities:* "Where there is true spirituality there is a beauty and harmony in human relationships." That assertion emanated from the crucible of his own painful experiences as a participant in the tremendous conflict within Protestantism early in this century. The conflict, sometimes referred to as the Fundamentalist-Modernist Controversy, was so intense that it divided believers, resulting in the establishment of new denominations.

Reflecting on his experience years later, Schaeffer acknowledged that although he and others of similar persuasion had a great concern for the truth, they did not have an equal concern to love others. As a matter of fact, the cumulative effect of problems and conflict encountered during his ministry brought him to the brink of despair. After several months of secluded thought and prayer, he emerged with a new understanding of spirituality—a spirituality that rejected the ugly meanness he had so often encountered. This true spirituality clothed itself in peace and harmony, issuing from genuine love—which he had come to realize was the true mark of Christianity.

Schaeffer was right. The brokenness of our fragmented, hurting world, a world inflicted with a traumatic loss of community and unable to heal itself, presents an extraordinary opportunity to demonstrate the power of the gospel, the great love of God incarnated in Jesus Christ. For Christ's love brings forgiveness and reconciliation. His love also obligates us to try to eradicate the estrangement and hostility that is so ubiquitous and pervasive.

What can be done about it? Try to understand rather than criticize and condemn. That means making an effort to get acquainted, listen, and understand. To do that you have to get inside the other person's world, and this is more difficult than you may think. I was struck by Steven Covey's confession that it was only after an extended sabbatical in Hawaii that he began to understand a long-standing point of tension between himself and his wife. It hinged on her determined allegiance to buy certain brand-name appliances. During their relaxed days together he discovered, through casual conversations about their past, that her allegiance was tied to her childhood experiences, namely to the loyalty and generosity her father's company had extended to him during the years of the Great Depression. The company helped preserve the family business.

Because she loved her father so much and knew what the company had done to help him, she felt compelled, although she was not consciously aware of it, to demonstrate that same loyalty to her father's company years after her father had died. Once Covey realized this, he had a new attitude toward this issue. There are many ways in which we similarly aggravate and alienate one another. These won't change unless we take the time to get to know each other well enough to see why such differences exist and to find ways to overcome them.

Our Lord can help us overcome the things that divide us. With his help we can take small but real steps toward healing. For this to happen we must genuinely want to love and forgive those who have hurt us. Knowing how easily our overtures can be misconstrued, it is all the more necessary to be patient and to persevere in the relationship rather than be discouraged or alienated by less than the desired or expected response. When the love of Christ guides our thoughts and actions, we may discover a new capacity to love and honor others so that a new winsomeness and beauty will characterize our relationships rather than rejection, anger, or hatred.

Several years ago I was part of an audience that witnessed an emotional confession from two Christian parents who told us about a harrowing experience with their son. As a very young fellow he professed faith in Christ and seemed to be powerfully directed toward a missionary career. Following his education, for one reason or another, he was distracted from this calling and his interests were directed elsewhere. He moved to another city in order to take a job. Then, with the passage of time, he began to do things that were incompatible with his family upbringing and his earlier Christian profession. Finally, in considerable turmoil, the young man phoned his brother to tell him how messed up his life had become and how he was now confronted by a new and unexpected problem. He discovered that he had AIDS. He knew he did not have long to live. He needed help. There was nowhere else to turn.

Stunned by this revelation, his brother asked, "Have you talked to Dad?" To which he replied, "No, I am not sure I can because I know how badly I have disappointed and hurt him." Then he described repeated efforts to find help at churches in his city, but when those churches found out about his gay lifestyle, he became unwelcome. Church doors had been slammed shut. At his brother's request, he decided to call home and tell his father about his condition. With a halting voice, hardly knowing how or where to begin, he told his father how embarrassed and ashamed he was to admit what had happened. Once he began to talk, the story flowed like a river—it was absolutely unstoppable. When he finished explaining everything, his father asked, "Son, do you remember the story of the prodigal?" The son replied, "Of course." He said, "Like that father, I am urging you to come home. We love you and we will help you."

Listening to those parents pour out their hearts, I heard God's message of forgiveness and reconciliation in a fresh way, especially regarding those whom we may find repugnant, because I found myself upset with the church for shunning him. The truth is that we are surrounded by people who have broken God's laws. We constantly encounter their pain, hurt, and alienation. Some of them are more unacceptable to us than others. But our response must be to reach out and invite all of them to come home to the Savior, who offers forgiveness and reconciliation. They need to come home to begin the healing and find a better life. When they do, we cannot afford to slam the door in their faces.

There has been enough bashing and beating, enough war and bloodshed. There has been too much criticism and condemnation. It is time to speak of grace. It is time to speak of love and mercy, to speak of the astonishing love of the Father who gave his Son as the perfect sacrifice for those who hated him and were his enemies so they can be forgiven and reconciled to him.

Pray for the meanness of this world, with its frustrations, fighting, and war. Someday the lion will lie down with the lamb, and with the dawning of that great day we shall gather in heaven as a vast crowd from every nation, tribe, people, and language, standing before the throne and worshiping him forever (Rev. 5:9). What a day of rejoicing that will be!

If you believe these things, then it's time for reconciliation. Take that step toward peace and harmony. Let it begin right now right here with you. Practice what Jesus commanded: "Therefore, if you are offering your gift at the altar and there remember that your brother has something against you, leave your gift there in front of the altar. First go and be reconciled to your brother; then come and offer your gift" (Matt. 5:23–24 NIV).

Chapter 15

Multicultural Attitudes

LEROY GAINEY
Matthew 5:1–10

The one thing that all people want, regardless of race or cultural background, is happiness. Jesus handled the situation, in this instance, where people had come from all over the region looking for happiness, representing numerous races, cultures, ages, and genders. They were all looking for a quick fix for getting answers to brokenness in the hope that this would lead to happiness. Happiness could be defined in this instance as "having your problems solved."

The only issue here is that new problems will occur, and if you base your happiness on not having any problems, the basis for your happiness

LEROY GAINEY *is associate professor of church growth and practical theology at Golden Gate Baptist Theological Seminary and also senior pastor-teacher of First Baptist Church, Vacaville, California. He holds degrees from Clark Atlanta University (B.A.), Interdenominational Theological Center (M.Div.), and Syracuse University (Ph.D.). A native of New York City, Dr. Gainey has had a distinguished career in pastoral ministry and community service, including a special internship with President Jimmy Carter. At Golden Gate, he has designed an African-American studies concentration to equip leaders to minister in African-American churches and communities, and is the chairperson for the Christian Education department. He has lectured on multicultural ministry and intercultural leadership development in many settings. He also serves as vice president of the National Task Force on Race and Reconciliation of the Southern Baptist Convention. Dr. Gainey's work on behalf of racial reconciliation was recently featured on an NBC network documentary.*

won't be strong or lasting. Jesus knows that quick-fix answers for life's problems, no matter who you are, are not good enough. Thus, Jesus called his disciples to himself and taught them principles to teach others, even races and cultures distant from their own, on how to have real happiness, how to be really satisfied. Jesus knew that he would need more than a committee for this task. Jesus would need a team!

Achieving a real state of happiness and being satisfied can look somewhat different, depending on the culture of your origin. In some cultures, money and material items define happiness. This is clearly seen in what is done with any "abundance" that is gained on top of the abundance that you already have. The false gospel of "name it and claim it, blab it and grab it" comes down to false prosperity and health, and it isn't really satisfying. Generally speaking, the abundance is put toward more of what you already have (for example, more cars, houses, investments, making more money). Thus, happiness is based upon the material things and additional material things you can add to your collection of things. You can build a mountain of such things, but these won't provide the happiness and satisfaction that come only from submission to Christ.

Others put their happiness and being satisfied into their careers. This category is characteristic of academic degrees, promotions, trophies, and other acclimates. John Thompson, the former coach of the nationally renowned collegiate basketball team, the Georgetown Hoyas, said that he kept a deflated basketball on his desk. Whenever new recruits came to see him, he would tell them that a basketball holds nine pounds of air. Do you want to trust your life to nine pounds of air?

Mr. Thompson meant that there is much more to life than basketball or the achievements you might gain from playing the game of basketball. All of life has somewhat of a "game" element attached to it. The Georgetown basketball team consisted of all

African-American players. Thompson was trying to get the players to see that there was more to life in regard to happiness and being satisfied than basketball. There is more to life in regard to happiness and being satisfied than any "game" you might excel in.

Soon after he became a Christian, the great professional football player Dion Sanders was asked, "Who are you now?" Dion responded, "Who is anyone when the lights are off and they are no longer calling your name? That's when you discover what real happiness and being satisfied is!" For Dion real happiness and being satisfied was being one of Christ's children and loving the Lord with all of his heart.

Many African-American athletes were denied the opportunity to play national sports until Jackie Robinson broke the color barrier in baseball. That picture has changed greatly over the years. African Americans now dominate in numbers and playing positions in basketball, football, and baseball. The problem is we've been victims of the "Jones" syndrome. The African-American athlete, as I see it, has not done much more, to a conspicuous degree, than buy more houses . . . more cars . . . more clothes . . . more playthings, and the great causes of humanity are still not addressed for all people (poverty, new businesses, greater institutions that promote racial harmony).

This isn't to say that some things aren't happening. You do hear of many athletes promoting their faith in Christ and many positive practices. But we have seen an obvious missing of the point by "conspicuous consumption" on the part of many new athlete millionaires. We don't know where many of them stand through the communication of their values, but their lifestyles say a lot.

We are still crying the blues concerning not having access to certain jobs in the front office. With the combined millions-plus salaries that athletes earn, they could own their own teams if they worked together. Happiness and being satisfied, sought after in careers and human self-promotion, is indeed a lost cause as much as it was for players of Anglo or other racial stock.

There are still others who seek happiness and being satisfied through drugs and chemical dependency. Addiction cares not about race, gender, culture, or physical and emotional challenge. I've never known anyone who has found the thing that all people seek for here. Chemical addictions end up in making you, and the people around you, miserable. After a brief initial high, you become a slave to the chemical.

Jesus pulled his team of disciples to the side to teach and mentor them on the fine art of empowering persons for the purpose of having a relationship and serving God. Jesus' teaching is a powerful reminder that becoming a "friend" of God and serving him is the only way to real happiness and being satisfied. God is pleased with us when we submit our lives and wills to him by allowing Christ to dwell in us. Jesus gave his disciples, and us, eight principles for training every human how to have real happiness for eternity.

Principle 1: "Blessed are the poor in spirit, for theirs is the kingdom of heaven" (Matt. 5:3 NIV).

I grew up in the Bronx, New York. My family was one of the millions of African Americans who migrated from the states of South Carolina, North Carolina, and Virginia to the area of the state of New York known as Harlem. The mass migration was due to young men returning from World War II who faced harsh racism from Anglo Americans living in those states mentioned above as well as others. The races, for the most part, fought beside each other overseas, but they came back to hostile environments in the southern United States where most of these young men came from. Their home states not only refused to recognize the contribution they had made in defending their country; they lynched and harassed them, designed segregated public schools and accommodations, and killed their children.

Because of what I experienced personally as a poor black male living in a housing project, the last word I wanted to associate with my name was "poor." If I could ever get out of the Bronx, New York, I thought, I could escape poverty forever. In reading this biblical text, I was faced with the dilemma of being "poor" as a state of happiness and well-being. It was a hard verse for me to accept. After doing a word study on "poor in spirit" in this context, I discovered that the phrase means "happy are they who are empty of themselves." The word *poor* has two connotations: "*penes*," where we get the word *pennies;* and "*p'tochos,*" which means to "not have anything." The word *psuche* in this context is translated "spirit," meaning "natural self." Generally, the word *pneuma* is translated as "spirit." This refers to a person who is born again of the Spirit. This spirit doesn't exist in the natural (not born-again) state. One would never expect those who are "born again" to become "poor in spirit."

The phrase "kingdom of heaven" (*baslicia oranous*) means "the royal place or realm where God lives." Those who completely empty themselves of "self" (being absorbed with self),and accept a better self (Holy Spirit-led life) will indeed have a guaranteed place in God's kingdom and, along these same lines, will have real happiness. All of the people who enter God's kingdom, regardless of color, gender, culture, or disability, must submit to the only One who didn't need to empty himself, because he was God in the form of Jesus. Now, at this point, having the guarantee of the kingdom of heaven as my eternal destiny, each day I gladly hand over the rest of myself for Jesus to transform. Thus, Jesus is not only my Savior; he is my model for living "poor in spirit." This first principle is essential and foundational for all that follows about the way to happiness.

A good example of how this looks in actuality is the difference between a wild horse and a tamed horse. A wild horse doesn't want to be controlled, doesn't want to submit to the owner. The tamed horse, though clearly the same animal on the outside, has given over its will (self) to the rider. The tamed horse is "poor in spirit." The wild horse is "spirited" or full of himself. Christ doesn't want to break our spirit; he simply wants all human creatures to turn themselves over to Jesus (our example) for a relationship with God. This is the beginning formula for happiness and being satisfied.

Principle 2: "Blessed are those who mourn, for they will be comforted" (Matt. 5:4 NIV).

The word *mourn* (*pentheo*) actually means "to shed real tears, to cry." This crying or grief is primarily on the inside. Any life led by the Creator is a much better life than one led by the creature (man). When I see a life that has not found the "poor in spirit" life, it makes me cry. When I see a dead life, I grieve on the inside. That's why I'm evangelical. I hate to see human life living less than its capabilities. This impacts my happiness and being satisfied. There are many sad pictures of living. The worst example is racism. In this instance I fool myself into believing I am better than other people because I am a different color. Color of skin will never make anyone truly happy. Skin doesn't have that ability.

Someone has said that human beings cost God about $1.37 to make. If humans could do it even bionically, it would cost billions. God uses about $1.37 worth of dust to make each human. Humans buy million-dollar houses so $1.37 can live in it. The same humans buy $40,000 cars so $1.37 can ride in them. And then some humans won't talk to each other because one is a different color of dust. How stupid!

Once you've experienced real happiness in knowing who you are and whose you are, it is difficult not to want others, no matter who they are, to experience the real joy you have discovered. It still makes me cry to see any race, culture, or gender of people without Jesus.

Crying over our hurts is a gift from God that allows the human creature to deal with stress caused by conditions that are beyond our control. We can do something, along with crying, that will help God in his work. We can join God by allowing him to use us as colaborers in his redemptive mission. We don't have the final word in this matter. We don't know who will respond. Hopefully, we won't let some historical or traditional experience of racial pain and suffering keep us from experiencing the real happiness that comes only through a relationship with God.

Principle 3: "Blessed are the meek, for they will inherit the earth" (Matt. 5:5 NIV).

The word "meek" (*praos*) is often confused with terms such as "weak." "Meek" means to have self-control. Maybe a better description is "Spirit-controlled." Meek people are the ones who will inherit the earth. They get angry at sin, not at people. Spirit-controlled persons use restraint in their sex lives, in their financial dealings, in their food and chemical intake. Ethnocentrism is a problem that all races experience. There are times when any person will allow racial pride to take center stage. Decisions based only on race suggest that the person isn't living a "Spirit-controlled life." A Holy Spirit-controlled life will get angry at sin, but will love the sinner.

When the "self" is in control, then the Spirit can't control. Martin Luther King Jr. courageously addressed the evil of those who tried to control the lives of others. Such people had to be confronted on the basis of God's standard of biblical righteousness and freedom for all humans. God is the only one who owns a person. No person has the right or authority to own another human being. People who are full of themselves will not live a Spirit-filled life unless they are held accountable. All humans need accountability to be meek.

Principle 4: "Blessed are those who hunger and thirst for righteousness, for they will be filled" (Matt. 5:6 NIV).

Hunger and thirst are basic needs of all people. Hunger and thirst are no respecters of persons. Abraham Maslow in his "hierarchy of needs" theory suggests that these basic human drives in all people are great for motivation. Righteousness (*dikaiosune*) means "standard of thinking"! People who don't have a clear understanding of biblical "right thinking" will create their own humanly devised substandard.

The craving of every human being is to be treated with respect, to be treated fairly. Jesus said there are two great commandments. The first is to love God. The second is to love our fellow human beings. The craving for righteousness, once filled, will drive a person to see that craving filled in other people. The hungering and thirsting is never for selfish righteousness. It is always accomplished by sharing this precious food with others who are hungry for the same right thinking. The promise of God to all who share his righteousness with all people "unto the ends of the earth" is that he will satisfy their deepest hungers.

Principle 5: "Blessed are the merciful, for they will be shown mercy" (Matt. 5:7 NIV).

The term for *mercy* (*eleemon*) means to step into someone else's shoes, to experience their experience. This means to feel empathetic, but also to do something about another's plight. Jesus did this for all of us. When we experience this kind of mercy, it is because Jesus is living inside our lives. What an awesome feeling to "feel" what others who are hurting feel. Mercy that knows how another person feels is like a powerful magnet. People who are hurting are drawn to others who know their hurt. I've never seen a drowning person discriminate on the basis of race! The one concern is, "Can you swim?" Jesus is able to save any drowning person. We don't need to work for Christ. We need to allow Christ to work through us. Christ has mercy enough for all the drowning people of the world.

Choose Christ and become a part of his family by adoption. The Book of Ruth is a great example of how Christ accomplished his work. In chapter 4 we find the story of the "kinsman redeemer." Boaz, who was from a different culture than Ruth, stepped into the shoes of the nearest kinsman. He was given the right to marry Ruth and assume responsibility for Ruth and Naomi as part of his family. Jesus, our nearest kinsman, has "stepped into our shoes" and paid our debt. Jesus, the eternal Son of the Father, has become our elder brother. His merciful act has redeemed us and set us free.

All of us—black, white, red, brown, and yellow—need this kind of mercy. No person can manufacture this kind of mercy and extend it to someone else. We don't possess this ability. An offering must be given, and we don't possess an offering that measures up to the standard. I could search the world over for someone to extend me this mercy, but I will never find it. If Jesus can't give it to me, I can't get it. My state remains unchanged. I'm on my way to hell. Hell is a place where no mercy is shown. I do believe that Christ's mercy is real and abundant to all humans. If we were given a pedigree German shepherd puppy, even if we didn't like dogs, we would know we had something of value. Even if we didn't want the dog, we would still treat the dog with the respect of a pedigree. Humans are worth more than dogs or anything else. Jesus died for humans not to make them valuable. Jesus died for humans because they *are* valuable!

Humans are the most powerful creatures on the earth. There is nothing that we don't have the potential of doing. We can build spacecrafts, design complicated computers, even find germs that cause diseases and are invisible to the naked eye. The only thing we cannot do is hand out "grace." Humans don't have the ability to save another human being. Jesus told the disciples that they would do greater things than he had done. Jesus has kept his word. The only thing reserved for him and kept out of our reach is the ability to save. All humans are kings, rulers, and priests. But there is a KING of KINGS, RULER of RULERS, a PRIEST of PRIESTS, and that is JESUS.

Principle 6: "Blessed are the pure in heart, for they will see God" (Matt. 5:8 NIV).

The term *pure* (*katharos*) means that something is 100 percent that element and no mixture with any other element. The term *heart* (*kardia*) is generally translated as the seat of emotions. A person who is pure in his or her emotions toward another person of the opposite sex has no distractions, dual interests, no two-timing, etc. This kind of love is best pictured by marriage between a man and a woman, "pure in heart."

The home we establish here on earth with our spouses is second in importance only to our eternal home with Jesus. Homes take work to establish. Someone can give you a house, but if you don't know how to make a home, you can tear up even the most beautiful house. Jesus commands us to take the Good News into all the world, to all kinds of people (*ethne*). Houses can come in many different colors. Christian homes only come in one color, "red." The blood of Christ is the purest cleanser anywhere for anybody.

People often brag on the fact that they come from "pure-bred" stock. They can trace their family back to Jefferson Davis, or Confederate soldiers, or Africa. To some individuals, personal esteem and self-concept are tied to the bloodline. They can look back to a human image that gives them great pride. All Christians are brothers and sisters through adoption. You can be all different colors and still be brothers and sisters through adoption into the same family. Adoption is a legally binding contract, giving all rights and privileges to the children equally.

The greatest consequence of this relationship is seeing Christ face-to-face. When I'm away from my wife, Cheryl, for any extended period, I can't wait to get back to see her face-to-face. But we also have new brothers and sisters from all different races and cultures. And one day, at the resurrection, I will get to see them too—all those who have died in Christ.

Principle 7: "Blessed are the peacemakers, for they will be called sons of God" (Matt. 5:9 NIV).

The Old Testament word for *peace* is *shalom*, which meant relational peace with other people. The Israelites experienced great tensions with other races around them. There were few periods of peace. Often the disturbance of the peace was sent by God as punishment for worshiping idols and other acts of disobedience to God's Word. The New Testament word for *peace* is *eirene*. *Eirene* means to have peace within, individual peace. Internal and eternal peace within can be experienced only through Jesus Christ. Outside of Christ, one can never have lasting peace within, the kind of peace that is worth more than silver or gold, houses or land, and things you can wear. Peace between people and nations can be achieved only when we realize who we are and to whom we belong.

History is filled with examples of how human beings have subjected one another to inhuman treatment. In the history of the United States, African Americans had their humanity taken from them by law, despite the fact that they were the heirs of great ancient African dynasties (Songhai, Mali, Timbuktu, Egypt, Ethiopia), all producers of advanced civilizations. Many other people groups also have a history of oppression, including Native Americans, Japanese, Hawaiians, Jews, Italians, etc. The efforts of some people to "control" others (e.g., by slavery or annihilation) can never yield peace. Peace between humans is possible only through Christ and submission to his Word.

The Bible teaches that human conflict and tension are rooted in sin (Gen. 3). Someone wants more power than someone else. Someone wants something that someone else has and exercises power over the other person to get it. But "children of God" have a powerful peace within them far greater than any power in the world. Jesus Christ allows humans to become partners in "peacemaking" with him.

One of the biggest mistakes a Christian can make is to think that lasting peace can be negotiated without the parties accepting Christ. Introducing Christ into the equation is the element that makes the difference. Christians are containers (vessels) for the Prince of Peace (Christ). Don't run from the opportunity to release Christ into a conflict situation. Preach his peace, sing his peace, teach his peace, write of his peace, dramatize his peace, communicate Christ in any way you can! He is the Prince of Peace. When Christ is acknowledged in any situation, the potential for peace has just been increased a hundredfold.

Principle 8: "Blessed are those who are persecuted because of righteousness, for theirs is the kingdom of heaven" (Matt. 5:10 NIV).

We shouldn't be surprised when people without Christ persecute others who know him. Satan is doing what comes natural to him. If you accept Christ and take his offer to use you seriously, persecution is coming. Persecutors against Christ are found everywhere. Taking the Good News into all the world is the most effective way to work against persecution.

There is a place promised to us where persecution does not exist. We can't get to heaven until God is ready for us to come, but we can rest assured that heaven is already ours. Heaven is a home that is worth all the persecution any Christian will go through. In the righteous army of God, we are all kings (rulers), serving under Christ who is the King of kings. Christ teaches us how to behave as a king in his kingdom. And he will show us how to stand up against persecution.

One of the talk shows recently featured a discussion of rap music and the First Amendment constitutional rights. All the guests on this show promoted music that degraded women and themselves. It appeared that the entire audience was on this same track when someone in the audience, who couldn't have been more than fifteen years old, stood up against the kind of lyrics that are demonic. The entire audience turned against her, and she sat down with her head down. I grabbed the face of my television and told her to "stand up for Jesus for righteousness' sake."

We can have happiness, and keep it, if we accept the strength and guidance of God through Jesus Christ. No human being can give you these important eternal elements of life. Your spouse can't give it to you, your children can't, your career can't, "we-are-the-world songs" can't. Only Jesus can!

Accept Christ into your life now and receive God's free gift tailored just for you. Accept Christ into your life and follow him. Christians aren't happy and satisfied because they follow a set of doctrines and values. Christians are happy and satisfied because they follow Christ. Christ is the living Word and the author of the written Word. Trust Christ with your life and be on the road to eternal happiness and satisfaction. Christ stands at the door of your life, and he is knocking, asking that you let him in to lead and guide you. There is a critical point when God has spoken to you, and that point is your response. The foundation for happiness and satisfaction is pleasing Christ and making this your greatest priority. *Immanuel!*

Conclusion

A young man was called to his first church in rural Georgia. The church building was literally located in the woods. There were fifty members, but on a good attendance Sunday, there were ten people. A business meeting brought many of the members out to consider a proposal from the young pastor to move the church fellowship to a new location where there was a large constituency of people—all different kinds of people. A motion was presented by a deacon, whose family tradition was embedded in the history of the pews and posts of the church. Thus stay at its present location in the woods. The motion was seconded and open for discussion. One little old lady, also a long-time member, ask to amend the motion. She said, "I motion that we give the deacon the pews and the posts so dear to him and let's move on." I agree with the little old lady. Today's ministry calls for reaching all the people of God. Let's move on!

Chapter 16
God Shows No Favoritism (And Neither Should We!)
CHARLES T. CARTER
Acts 10:34–35; James 2:1, 9

Ever since God made "the first brothers," Cain and Abel, "different" from one another and Cain killed Abel, prejudice has been a seething problem to mankind. Though hopefully much progress has been made in America since the Supreme Court ruling in 1954 and the Civil Rights Act in 1964, prejudice and racism are still very much "real life" issues.

Evidence of this is a recent feature article entitled "Huge Police Force Helps Keep Peace at KKK Rally" in the largest daily newspaper in Alabama.[1] A few years earlier an editorial in *The Birmingham Post-Herald* was labeled "Race Still Divides."[2] Just days after this, an eastern suburb of the state's largest city was disrupted as an African-

CHARLES T. CARTER *is retired senior pastor of Shades Mountain Baptist Church in Birmingham, Alabama, a congregation he served faithfully as pastor for twenty-six years. He holds degrees from Samford University (B.A.; D.D.) and the Southern Baptist Theological Seminary (M.Div.). A superb Bible teacher and evangelistic preacher, Dr. Carter has spoken in numerous churches and conferences throughout the Southern Baptist Convention and around the world. He has served as a trustee of the International Mission Board of the Southern Baptist Convention, and as president of the Alabama Baptist State Convention (1988–1990). He was chairman of the Resolutions Committee at the 1995 Southern Baptist Convention in Atlanta, which adopted the historic resolution on racial reconciliation, included in this book as an appendix.*

American family awoke on a Monday morning to find the hated racial slur "Die N_____" scrawled across their front porch in chocolate syrup.³

Enough has been said to substantiate that as Christians move into a new millennium, we still face challenges to deal with racist attitudes both *inside* and *outside* the church. These attitudes infiltrate *all* races and *all* classes, though the prime focus of this message is on reconciliation among blacks and whites.

The dictionary defines *racism* as "a belief that racial differences produce an inherent superiority of a particular race."⁴ The word *race* (as applied to people) does not appear in the Bible, nor does the term *racism*. However, the Bible *does* give clear guiding principles to follow in dealing with the age-old problem of prejudice.

The destructive hostility that still exists in places in our culture between races (such as blacks and whites) is essentially no different in substance than that which fragmented the early church as seen in our texts in Acts 10 and James 2. Jews and Gentiles literally hated and despised one another. Even one as close to the Lord Jesus as Simon Peter, a devout Jew, had to go through a complete spiritual and attitudinal metamorphosis (Acts 10:9–16) to come to accept non-Jews as brothers in Christ.

After his vision on the roof in the home of Simon the tanner in Joppa (Acts 10:9–16), where he was instructed, "Do not call anything impure that God has made clean" (v. 15 NIV), and after God validated Peter's preaching to the Gentiles at the house of Cornelius by pouring out the Holy Spirit upon them (Acts 10:45), Peter was convinced that, indeed, "God does not show favoritism" (Acts 10:34 NIV)—nor should we!

What Peter painfully yet convincingly learned in the first century, many believers in the twentieth century still must grasp. As we evaluate dealing with the matter of racial prejudice, let us examine four areas: (1) some personal observations, (2) some factual considerations, (3) some biblical information, and (4) some practical exhortations.

I. Some Personal Observations

So often the passionate pleas to break down racial barriers are rejected by those in our southern culture as coming from "outsiders who don't understand." This message is *not* coming from "an outsider"; I am a "son of the South," a product of our culture with all of its pluses along with some of its minuses. Changes directly related to "race" have affected virtually every area of my past.

A. The *home* in which I grew up through my teenage years is now occupied by an African-American family.

B. The *schools* I attended (elementary and high school) are either non-existent or almost completely attended by blacks.

C. The *church* in which I was saved, baptized, called to preach, and licensed and ordained to the gospel ministry (the former Calvary Baptist Church) is now a wonderful black congregation, the Macedonia 17th Street Baptist Church.

D. The *city* in which I was reared and educated—Birmingham, Alabama—at times has been in the forefront of racial tension. I sat at Legion Field football stadium on Easter Sunday afternoon in 1963 and listened to Billy Graham preach to an integrated audience in a one-day rally. His presence and purpose was to try to alleviate some of the red-hot racial tension that was festering. His sincerity and integrity along with the genuineness of the simple gospel he proclaimed forever made an impression on my young life—and certainly helped our city through a difficult moment.

E. My *first pastorate* as a teenage preacher was assaulted by the deadly venom of misguided prejudice. At a Saturday night youth rally there, on November 26, 1955, ten hooded Ku Klux Klansmen walked in and disrupted a public worship service! The next morning I was on a "coast-to-coast" radio broadcast at the local station (from one coast of the county to the other!). I stayed up all night preparing a biblical sermon on James 2 with the same essential theme as this message—that "God is no respecter of persons." In retrospect today, I realize, though I "spoke the truth," I did *not* "speak the truth in love" (Eph. 4:15). In the vernacular, I "blistered their hides"; I was so hurt and so angry!

F. In my *final pastorate*, which I assumed in 1971 and where I remained for more than twenty-six years, I explained in a public church-wide forum, prior to their calling me, that as a Christian minister, *never* would I discourage or reject someone from church membership solely on the basis of their "different" ethnic origin. A unanimous call was extended. Less than two years later, however, when "the first black" (as some said) came for membership, some of my dearest friends "left the church," stating they could never support a church that would accept "those kinds of people." Again I was deeply hurt, but I trust my pastoral letter to them reflected more maturity and love than had my zeal without knowledge (see Rom. 10:2) response to the KKK eighteen years earlier.

All of this autobiographical account is to validate that this message is not coming from the heart of a naïve, uninformed "outsider." I have "been there—done that"! In the midst of racial tension I have personally seen Christians at their *worst* and at their *best!*

More than a hundred years ago, during the tensions of the Civil War, there was a need for Christians to say, "God shows no favoritism." Nearly fifty years ago, when the KKK was disrupting public worship services, there was a need for Christians to say, "God shows no favoritism." Though much healthy and productive progress has been made, still today, at the turn of the new millennium, there still remains a need for Christians of all races to proclaim, "God shows no favoritism"—nor should we!

II. Some Factual Considerations

Grasping the cultural milieu in which we must function can help us comprehend the complexity of the situation as we try to demonstrate the impartiality of God.

Generally. According to world demographics, some 94 percent of the population lives *outside* the United States. Most of these are nonwhite.

In my "little part of the world" where I live, the African-American population is as follows:

- 1.1% Vestavia Hills (my municipality)
- 7.8% Shelby County (my nearest neighbor south)
- 12% United States (my nation)
- 25% Alabama (my state)
- 35% Jefferson County (my county)

Religiously. In our nation, 40 percent of the African-American population are Baptists. In Alabama, there are four Black Baptist state conventions (some say five), with 1,170 churches and approximately 400,000 members.

Educationally. More than 50 percent of African Americans have not finished high school. Most African-American pastors have not had college or seminary training. Relatively few young black ministers are in training currently in college or seminary; yet 1,500 black churches become vacant each year.

Socially. Black unemployment is usually double that of whites. In the area of crime, 28 percent of all arrests are black, though only 12 percent of the population is black. The most recent statistics across the nation reveal that this 12 percent of African Americans are responsible for:

- 55% of murders,
- 53% of thefts,
- 47% of rapes, and
- 62% of illegitimate births.

The above facts often compound our efforts to overcome racism. They also cause many to stereotype *all* African Americans. I often say to my white friends, "We must show love for *all* people, regardless of their behavior, as our heavenly Father *always* does to us." To my black friends I say, "To help your peers be respected, you must urge and encourage them to live respectably in their social behavior, as must whites." Fortunately, improvements have been made in some of these trends within the last several years. Beyond this, increasingly, African Americans are achieving executive-level leadership in certain major corporations.[5]

III. Some Biblical Information

What does the Bible teach that can guide us in dealing with racism in whatever form it manifests itself? Indeed, what is the theological tapestry that forms the background to our acceptance of *all* people, regardless of their ethnicity?

To answer these questions, let us examine scriptural teachings in four areas: God, Man, Jesus, and the Church.

Concerning God

God created all (Acts 17:24–27). The Bible teaches us that "God . . . made the world and everything in it. . . . From one man he made every nation of men. . . . God did this so that men would seek him and perhaps . . . find him, though he is not far from each one of us" (NIV). This divine creative act of God is the ultimate source of all persons, regardless of our various ethnic origins. The original intent, purpose, and plan of God was that *all* those made in his image would enjoy fellowship with him as well as with one another. Just as it is impossible to think of human parents, having shared with God in creating multiple children, loving one child more than or less than the others, it is unconscionable to attribute such a posture to our loving heavenly Father! Yet, at its root, racism does just that.

God loves all (John 3:16). The best-loved verse in the Scriptures tells us, "God so loved *the world*" (NIV). As our children sing, "Red and yellow, black and white; they are precious in His sight." The genuine compassion of God reaches out to all people unselfishly, unconditionally, and unmotivatedly. He loves not "because of," but "in spite of"; he loves not because of what's in us, but because of what's in *him*—unconditional love. By his Spirit, whom he freely gives to every believer, he enables us to love in the same manner, regardless of "differences."

God reconciles all (2 Cor. 5:19). Paul teaches us in this passage that "God was reconciling *the world* to himself in Christ" (NIV). Not only are we given this *message* of reconciliation; there is committed to us the *ministry* of reconciliation. It is almost overwhelming to grasp the truth of 2 Corinthians 5:20, "We are . . . Christ's ambassadors, as though God were making his appeal through us" (NIV). Surely both this *message* and *ministry* of reconciliation would expel any residual bigotry in any form.

God shows favoritism to none (Acts 10:34–35). This, our initial text, shows Peter, a devout Jew with all the barnacles of accumulated prejudice against the Gentiles, coming to grasp, as a direct by-product of his vision given by God, that "God does not show favoritism but accepts men from every nation who fear him and do what is right" (NIV). Peter's life and ministry would never be the same again, nor will ours when we have a similar divine encounter, but we must be willing and open to *change.*

Concerning Man

All are made in the image of God (Gen. 1:26–27). The first book of our Bible tells us that God said, "Let us make man in our image. . . . So God created man in his own image" (NIV). Whatever the *imago dei* means, it certainly means that of all the animate beings on earth, *only man* has the capacity to have fellowship with God; and the other equally glorious truth is that *all* humans, *whatever their race*, have this God-given capacity! The privilege of communing with God in prayer, praise, and worship is open to *everyone*. God forbid anyone would ever arrogantly think they could usurp the authority to determine who could or could not do this, least of all when the litmus test was "the color of their skin"!

All have sinned (Rom. 3:23). The story of Adam in the early chapters of Genesis is the story of everyone's life—we "all have sinned." We are all sinners by *nature*; we have all confronted the *choice* of right and wrong, and have made the wrong choice; we have all put our choice into *practice* in deeds of rebellion against a holy God. As Paul said, "There is no one who does good, not even one" (Rom. 3:12 NIV), and "Jews and Gentiles alike are all under sin" (Rom. 3:9 NIV). All people of all races have one common problem—*sin*—and one common Savior—Jesus!

All who do God's will are brothers (Mark 3:35). Despite our depravity in sin, *all* who receive the free "gift of God," eternal life, through faith in the Lord Jesus Christ (cf. Rom. 6:23) come into the center of God's will and thereby become members of God's family. Our Lord said in Mark 3:35, "Whoever does God's will is my brother and sister" (NIV). By every means possible we as Christians must strive to permit this spiritual brotherhood to permeate our secular society. Later Jesus said, "By this all men will know that you are my disciples, if you love one another" (John 13:35 NIV).

Concerning Jesus

Certainly our theology of Christ underscores the universality of the gospel. In him, none were ever excluded.

He died for all (2 Cor. 5:15). One of Paul's simplest statements in his Corinthian correspondence was "He (Christ) died for all" (NIV). Later in that same chapter he says, "If *anyone* is in Christ, he is a new creation" (2 Cor. 5:17 NIV). With this concept as the bedrock of our gospel, how contradictory it would be for any Christian or church anywhere remotely to suggest that the only "accepted ones" are "our kind and color." This would be the epitome of arrogance and borders on being blasphemous. May it never happen!

He is Lord of all (Rom. 10:12). The same apostle (Paul) who called himself "the apostle to the Gentiles" (Rom. 11:13 NIV) also proclaimed, "There is no difference between Jew and Gentile—the same Lord is Lord of all and richly blesses all who call on him" (Rom. 10:12 NIV). The lordship of Jesus Christ stands at the very heart of our gospel. If he is the black man's Lord (and he is) and he is the white man's Lord (and he is), then automatically and instantaneously his lordship binds us together as brothers.

His Great Commission is to all (Matt. 28:19). As Jesus was about to ascend back to heaven, he uttered his last recorded earthly words to his followers and thereby spelled out their first and foremost responsibility—to "make disciples." Interestingly, the arena in which this commission is to be fulfilled is "all nations" (πάντα τὰ ἔθνη). To be monotheistic is to be missionary; and to be missionary (in the biblical sense) is to be all-inclusive in the invitation extended.

Concerning the Church

Addressing the racial division and hostility between Jew and Gentile while simultaneously showing how Christ dealt decisively at the cross with these matters, Paul says, "For he himself is our peace, who has made the two one and has destroyed the barrier, the dividing wall of hostility. . . . His purpose was to create in himself one new man out of the two, thus making peace" (Eph. 2:14–15 NIV). So much in our society outside the church fragments and divides the human family. In Christ and in his church, through what happened at the cross, there is peace and there is unity.

J. B. Phillips poignantly paraphrases a part of the above passage: "The war was over" (Phillips). May our local churches become outward manifestations of the truth of these words, demonstrating them in concrete reality. May our members learn that if they plan to sing in the Hallelujah Choir "up there," they must remember that choir practice starts "down here"—under the direction and tutelage of the Maestro, Jesus Christ, himself, who is "the chief cornerstone" (Eph. 2:20 NIV). He can take the *whiteness* of sopranos and the *blackness* of altos and the *yellowness* of tenors and the *redness* of basses and beautifully homogenize them *all* in heavenly music. Ideally, the church of the Lord Jesus Christ should be a microcosm of what heaven will be like, where everyone who has acknowledged "Jesus is Lord" is accepted as brothers in Christ.

IV. Some Practical Exhortations

Obviously, in conclusion, the practical question inevitably arises—"What can I do" to help implement racial reconciliation? Let us seek to answer this denominationally, ecclesiastically, and personally.

A. What Can Be Done Denominationally?

Because of my own background and experience, I must speak primarily from a Southern Baptist posture. At the 150th anniversary of the Southern Baptist Convention, in June of 1995, it was my privilege, at the request of convention president Dr. Jim Henry, to serve as chairman of the Resolutions Committee that presented a "Resolution on Racial Reconciliation."[6] This document was approved almost unanimously by the messengers present. Certainly this historic action spoke pointedly to some of our failures in the past as well as our goals for the future. However, as I said to the media immediately following this convention, it is relatively easy to pass a resolution (important as this is) within the protective walls of a convention hall; it is a completely different (and certainly more important) matter· to "translate" its truths into "flesh and blood" reality within the contexts of our multiple communities and churches.

This action made the front page of the *Wall Street Journal* as well as the *New York Times*. It is even more crucial that its truths capture the hearts and minds of our constituency, serving as a catalytic agent to implement needed changes in traditions, attitudes, and relationships. At least it was a major step in the right direction. Hopefully we can continue on that journey.

On a broader scale denominationally, in the early days of 1999 (January 8–11) delegates from thirty countries attended in Atlanta, Georgia, an international summit of Baptists Against Racism. It was sponsored by the Baptist World Alliance (BWA), a worldwide fellowship of Baptist unions and conventions based in Washington. Some of the sessions were held at the Ebenezer Baptist Church, home church of Dr. Martin Luther King Jr.

Delegates drafted a lengthy statement declaring a "decade to promote racial justice" beginning in 2000. Respective BWA unions were urged to promote efforts to eradicate racism. Specifically it called for Baptists to work for integrated worship and holistic evangelism as well as to reject paternalism by international missionaries.[7]

B. What Can Be Done Ecclesiastically?

At best, denominational groups can only issue official postures and pleas. The place "where the water hits the wheel" is in the local church and in the hearts of local church leadership. Still, Christian churches in the South are described as "the last rampart of segregation."[8] Local congregations can go a long way toward dismantling racist attitudes by engaging in intensive study, teaching, and preaching of the Bible on this issue. Hopefully spiritual growth can result, producing personal attitudinal changes so drastically needed. This also can lead to an "open door" policy of "whosoever will, may come" in response to the proclamation of the gospel message. To do this takes love, patience, tact, credibility, and Christlikeness on the part of leadership.

Another local church action might be pursuing the possibility of establishing ongoing partnerships across racial lines. A figure of no less stature than fellow Baptist and former President Jimmy Carter has suggested such action.[9] This could include informal church fellowships to "get to know one another." It could encompass pulpit exchanges between the respective pastors as well as joint worship services. In all of this a part of the purpose is to enable Christians of different races *really* to establish wholesome, healthy dialogue and relationships with one another. Bridges can be built enabling future shared ministries.

Having done this in a local setting, I can attest personally to the fact that it does work. Lasting friendships with people of other races have been established, along with an ongoing partnership of involvement in helping to foster strategic inner-city ministries.

C. What Can Be Done Personally?

One major step in eradicating racism personally is to *acknowledge* the problem of prejudice where it exists. So often people considering themselves to be "good Christians" (of all races) are oblivious to the existence of deep-seated prejudices. At other times we succumb to "stereotyping" certain persons or ethnic groups. Even those avoiding these dilemmas are not guiltless. A major problem I personally encounter regularly is finding myself being "prejudiced against prejudiced people"! So often, their spirit and disposition is mean—yet they are loved by God as much as we are, and we must try to respond to them with a spirit of *agape*.

A second personal step is to accept the authority of Holy Scripture (such as Acts 10:34–35 and James 2:1, 9) in the area of racism as much as in the area of the plan of salvation. We must be cautious not to read our biases and prejudices and traditions into the pure truth of the Word of God.

Finally, we can resolve to seek to apply "the royal law" (James 2:8), the ethic of Christian love, to all our interpersonal relationships. James plainly says, "If you really keep the royal law, . . . 'Love your neighbor as yourself,' you are doing right" (James 2:8 NIV). It could not be any clearer. To underscore the truth, the following verse says, "But if you show favoritism, you sin" (James 2:9 NIV).

To summarize:

As *individuals,* we can resolve to make planned, deliberate efforts really to "get to know" Christians of other races, establishing relationships and friendships with them, and letting them know we really do love and care.

As *families,* we can discuss with our children the problems of prejudice and the teachings of the Bible (such as the parable of the good Samaritan). We can teach them to be kind, thoughtful, and respectful to all people, regardless of their races. In our homes, by our words, actions, and attitudes, we can model how

Christians should act, devoid of racism. So often these feelings are "caught more than taught." At times we can learn from our children; frequently they have the least problem of all with prejudice. Often they have the ability just to "accept people as they are." May we learn from them!

As *churches,* we can support pastoral leadership that wants it to be known that no one is rejected from our Christian fellowship on the basis of color. We can put *substance* and *actions* behind the words of our resolutions. We can continue to proclaim the person of Jesus Christ as the cure for the deepest problems of mankind. Indeed, our gospel message is "amazing grace for every race"!

Reconciliation:
Two Biblical Studies

JAMES EARL MASSEY

EDITOR'S NOTE: On February 25–26, 1999, Dr. James Earl Massey spoke to the Meeting of U.S. Church Leaders at the renowned Cosmos Club in Washington, D.C. Composed of leaders of several major denominations in the United States, this group meets annually for discussion and fellowship. Dr. Massey spoke on the theme, "Reconciliation: Two Biblical Studies." We include here the text of his remarks both as a personal tribute to Dr. Massey himself and as a fitting conclusion to this volume on racial reconciliation.

The topic you have chosen, and to which you have asked me to respond from the perspective of the Holy Scriptures, is strategic and timely, for everywhere one looks, whether at life within America or at life across our world, conflicts between persons and groups are playing themselves out, with publicized, prolonged, and un-

civil struggling over differences—differences in values and ethics, differences in religious views, differences over land claims, territorial rights, political ends and a host of other fractious debates. Conflict holds center stage in our time and in all places, and voices of wisdom addressed to those involved in the fray—or the number of persons of good will to help quell the conflicts—are all too few. I applaud your concern to become more effective agents of our Lord as we face the issues and handle the living of these days as his people.

Addressing this august assemblage is both a joy and a challenge: a joy because as "people of The Book" we have a deep respect for what the Christian Scriptures have to say on the subject of reconciliation, as well as on all other subjects, and we have a mutual interest in listening anew as we explore the passages that deal with the subject chosen for this gathering; but the challenge before us all is in the task that awaits us after hearing the Word and seeing the path we must therefore take as it stretches out into territory fraught with the conflicts that occur when people meet, those conflicts we are called and sent to address in the name and power of him who is our peace.

In preparing for this assignment, I have had to do some fresh theological thinking based upon fresh exegetical work in some strategic New Testament passages. Based upon all this, some theological insights and practical applications that follow from them will be explored during our time together. As your Bible study leader this year, I take comfort in the fact that I am working with you who because of your training as well as your work form what James Barr has referred to as "an instructed theological public."[1]

In this first biblical study, then, I invite you to join me in re-exploring the major biblical passages regarding reconciliation, giving due attention to the terms the writers used, the contexts within which those terms were used, and the meanings to which we are heirs because of their received work. During the second study, I want to trace some lines of guidance that our first study will have brought to our attention, some lines of guidance that I am confident you will agree are crucial for our lives as we return to our labors as people of God.

I. Reconciliation: The New Testament Teachings

The first passage for consideration in treating what the New Testament teaches regarding reconciliation is found among the ethical instructions from our Lord, and it is located in Matthew's account of the Sermon on the Mount, Matthew 5:21–26. Before reading that section, let me remind you that it contains the first of the six bold antithetic imperatives from our Lord that reflect his authority as not only Moses's successor but Moses's superior. These six antitheses carry us to the very heart of what constitutes a truly righteous heart response in human experience; they tell us how the new life under the lordship of Christ surpasses life under the old laws of Moses, which explains the construction that is found in these teachings: "You have heard that it was said ... but I say to you."

The section from the Sermon on the Mount with which we are concerned here, Matthew 5:21–26, deals with anger, that strong human feeling of displeasure that at a belligerently wrathful stage can result in murder. Jesus offered instruction for his followers on how to handle anger before that stage of belligerency is reached. He also tells how anger can block a relationship with God. Here is the passage:

> **5:21** You have heard that it was said to those of ancient times, "You shall not murder"; and "whoever murders shall be liable to judgment."
>
> **5:22** But I say to you that if you are angry with a brother or sister, you will be liable to judgment; and if you insult a brother or sister, you will be liable to the council; and if you say, "You fool," you will be liable to the hell of fire.
>
> **5:23** So when you are offering your gift at the altar, if you remember that your brother or sister has something against you,
>
> **5:24** leave your gift there before the altar and go; first *be reconciled* to your brother or sister, and then come and offer your gift. (NRSV, emphasis mine)

Please note that the speaking of rash, insulting words to others, all selfish speaking out of intense feelings that are full of human wrath, even if those feelings have been provoked by someone's prior selfish action, is viewed by Jesus as not only a selfish response to the offending person but as a sinful deed in God's sight as well. Hostility is an activity of the heart, and those who wish to be accepted in peace by God must be serious about remaining at peace with humans. True worship is blocked whenever and as long as hostility rages within the heart against another human. As verses 23–24 state, reconciliation between the aggrieved parties must take place before God will accept our worship. Please note that the instruction is "be reconciled," meaning that the one who seeks to please God must take the initiative to remove whatever blocks a right relation with the other person. The verb used here is *diallagēthi* [aorist imperative passive of *diallassō*], a word that appears only here in the New Testament, and one of only four such terms used that mean "to restore or bring back into agreement or harmony a relation that has been broken or is at odds."

The second passage I call to your attention is found in Acts 7. The entire chapter reports Stephen the deacon's defensive speech to the Sanhedrin as its members sat in council against him as he witnessed about Jesus. As he engaged in historical retrospect, seeking to show that the history of their people pointed to the very happenings to which he was witness, Stephen recalled the life and times of Moses, the nation's great lawgiver, and how he had been readied for his role by growing up as a prince in Egypt, the place of their first and longest confinement. Then comes that section in the narrative:

> **7:23** When he was forty years old, it came into his heart to visit his relatives, the Israelites.
>
> **7:24** When he saw one of them being wronged, he defended the oppressed man and avenged him by striking down the Egyptian.
>
> **7:25** He supposed that his kinsfolk would understand that God through him was rescuing them, but they did not understand.

> **7:26** The next day he came to some of them as they were quarreling and tried to reconcile [*sunēllassen*] them, saying, "Men, you are brothers; why do you wrong each other?"
> **7:27** But the man who was wronging his neighbor pushed Moses aside, saying, "Who made you a ruler and a judge over us?
> **7:28** Do you want to kill me as you killed the Egyptian yesterday?" (NRSV)

It is not necessary to say anything more about that passage except to point out the word used in verse 26 for *reconcile:* It is the word *sunallassō*, and is a second New Testament term that I call to your attention. The imperfect form, *sunēllassen*, of that verb is used here in the report to indicate that Moses "tried to reconcile" the two recalcitrant brawling Hebrews.

A third passage that mentions reconciliation, using a third term, *katallassō*, is found in 1 Corinthians 7, and it is part of some instruction from Paul about the need to restore a lost or problem-threatened spousal relationship. Interestingly, this instruction will show an immediate dependence by Paul upon the sayings of Jesus about marriage. The ethics Paul taught actually reflect exact parallels at many points with the teachings of Jesus, and even when no parallel is evident, his judgments and recommendations to believers are understandably at one with the spirit of those teachings. In the instruction Paul gives in 1 Corinthians 7:10–11, it is quite clear that he has appropriated a known teaching of the Lord and passes it on in the interest of restoring a broken or fragmenting marriage relationship. It is possible that Paul appealed here to some fixed written record that he possessed, some form of sayings-collection that had been gathered because of controversies, questions about moral matters, and the meaning of certain passages from the Hebrew Bible (in its Septuagint translation, of course) that were important for instructing the believers. While that is possible and would explain so much, I cannot state that it was indeed the case, but the very fact that he could write "to the married I give this command—not I but the Lord" shows a strict knowledge about the Lord's words on the matter of spousal relations. Thus, Paul was not inventing new directions when he counseled:

> **7:10** To the married I give this command—not I but the Lord—that the wife should not separate [*mē chōristhēnai*] from her husband
>
> **7:11** (but if she does separate [*choristhe*], let her remain unmarried or else **be reconciled** [*katallagētō*] to her husband), and that the husband should not divorce his wife. (NRSV, emphasis mine)

Paul here addresses a Christian couple whose married life has for some reason become problematic and irksome or broken. His charge to them is based on the Lord's own teaching on the matter: do not divorce one another. The traditional teaching as reported in Matthew 5:32 and 19:9, and Mark 10:11 is reflected here. The family should remain in solidarity; if the wife insists upon leaving the marriage, she must remain single [*menetō agamos*], and the husband must not marry someone else during the separation. This command of Jesus that Paul quotes and applies regards the bond that marriage involves, and he reminds the couple that reconciliation should be their proper concern if that bond is placed under severe strain and they separate.

Katallassō, the word used here, in this third passage, is the most used word in the New Testament for reconciliation. The basic meaning of the Greek term is "to change, or exchange; to effect a change." This word is used exclusively by Paul among the New Testament writers, and always to help express and explain to his readers some of the meaning and effects of Christ's deed of dying for us on a cross. In the uses of this term on Paul's part, we are being instructed about the atonement, which in the words of Vincent Taylor, is "the work of God in Christ for man's salvation and renewal."[2]

The word *katallassō* denotes a relation, a relation that has undergone a change for the better. It is one word among many in a family of images that set forth to us the meaning of a changed relation. The changed relation is made possible by someone acting toward someone else with concern to effect that change. The image in the word shows something having been set aside or put down [*kata*]: an attitude, a grievance, a position, a deed, a distance, a result, in order to induce or bring about a change for the better. A new disposition is exhibited, a new stance is assumed, a new framework is established granting a rich togetherness where enmity and distance previously were the order. As used by Paul, the noun "reconciliation" [*katallagē*] reports something proffered to us by God (Rom. 5:8–11) and something experienced by us on the basis of the sacrificial death Jesus Christ underwent on our behalf (2 Cor. 5:17ff).

There is a fourth term used in the New Testament for reconciliation: it is the word *apokatallassō*, found at Ephesians 2:16 and Colossians 1:20, 22, and it is a part of the same theological message that the apostle Paul states regarding the meaning and effects of the death and resurrection of Jesus for those who believe on him. I will return to a treatment of this word and the verses in which it appears, but first I want to examine 2 Corinthians 5:16–21, that classic passage regarding reconciliation.

In 2 Corinthians 5:16–21, Paul is making a personal statement and an advisory claim. Having entered upon a new life-course through his converting contact with the risen Christ, and having undergone a full change of worldview thereby, Paul here states his reasons for the ministry at which he has long been engaged now: (a) He is part of a "new creation" inaugurated by being "in Christ" (= inhabiting a new sphere of reality); and (b) he has received a commission to announce to all that reconciling action of God in Christ by which that newness became possible.

It is helpful to point out that this statement on Paul's part is in defense of his ministry, which, as we see earlier in this letter, has been the subject under attack by some of his critics (2:14–7:4). The attitude of those critics toward him was not just suspicious but hostile and defiant (see 2:5–11; 7:12). Paul was no longer the Moses-follower (3:1–18), like his critics, but a Christ-follower; Paul knew that the promised New Age has already dawned, and he knew himself called by God to announce that fact and declare and expound upon the results and effects for all who believe.

Paul wrote as he did because he was concerned about two things: to keep trusting believers rightly informed about his ministry; and to become reconciled with those who were his detractors. Paul wanted his critics to be compatriots in Christ, to be in right relation with him again. As he sought to inform, influence, and win them, he became poetic, and his lyrical bent comes through in the hymnic statement we find in this great passage. Viewing the whole of life and humanity now through eyes touched by the risen Christ, Paul wanted his readers to be fully oriented to a new way of viewing him and all others as well. As he states it:

> **5:16** From now on, therefore, we regard no one from a human point of view; even though we once knew Christ from a human point of view, we know him no longer in that way.
>
> **5:17** So if anyone is in Christ, there is a new creation: everything old has passed away; see, everything has become new!
>
> **5:18** All this is from God, who reconciled [*katallazontos*] us to himself through Christ, and has given us the ministry of reconciliation [*katallagē*];
>
> **5:19** that is, in Christ God was reconciling [*katallassōn*] the world to himself, not counting their

trespasses against them, and entrusting the message of reconciliation [*katallagēs*] to us.

5:20 So we are ambassadors for Christ, since God is making his appeal through us; we entreat you on behalf of Christ, be reconciled [*katallagēte*] to God. **5:21** For our sake he made him to be sin who knew no sin, so that in him we might become the righteousness of God. (NRSV)

Please notice that Paul explains that God is the reconciler; God took the initiative, while the world, i.e., humankind, is the object of God's reconciling action. Christ is God's agent of reconciliation, and through Christ alone was that reconciliation made possible. "In Christ God was reconciling the world to himself," Paul declares in verse 19, and he urged his believing readers to join him in being reconciled in full in verse 20: "Be reconciled [*katallagēte*, aorist imperative passive] to God." What God initiated through grace and has proffered in love, we can experience through acceptance in faith and continuing obedience.

Romans 5:10–11 repeats the statement about what has been proffered and experienced:

5:10 For if while we were enemies, we were reconciled [*katēllagēmen,* aorist passive] to God through the death of his Son, much more surely, having been reconciled [*katallagentes,* aorist participle passive], will we be saved by his life. **5:11** But more than that, we even boast in God through our Lord Jesus Christ, through whom we have now received reconciliation [*katallagē*]. (NRSV)

Let us turn back now to the two passages I mentioned, Ephesians 2:16 and Colossians 1:20 and 22.

In Ephesians 2:16 we see Paul's discussion of reconciliation as it relates to the removal of the previous division that existed between Jews and Gentiles, a division based upon not just one but several separating factors: religious differences, legal differences, cultural differences, racial and social differences. In a bold and declarative announcement, Paul states that God's reconciling deed in Christ has changed that distancing division altogether and has made the two groups one in his sight:

> **2:13** But now in Christ Jesus you who once were far off have been brought near by the blood of Christ.
>
> **2:14** For he is our peace; in his flesh he has made both groups into one and has broken down the dividing wall, that is, the hostility between us.
>
> **2:15** He has abolished the law with its commandments and ordinances, that he might create in himself one new humanity in place of the two, thus making peace,
>
> **2:16** and might reconcile [*apokatallazē,* aorist subjunctive] both groups to God in one body through the cross, thus putting to death that hostility through it. (NRSV)

Then follows that grand peroration about the believing Gentiles' privileged participation, on equal footing, with believing Jews in God's "household," the church. Here we see a wider communal interest to God's reconciling deed in Christ, a wider social application of the effects of reconciliation. The God-ordained relationship between Christian believers, of whatever previous backgrounds, is not just one of harmony but a oneness where neither group is dominant nor subservient anymore. The fence that once stood between them is now down. Because believers are reconciled to God, they are also related to one another. A new set of criteria applies now for human relations in the Church. In church life social distance must no longer be the order, and a sense of oneness and equality must prevail when previously-honored differences seek to intrude themselves.

The last reference test is Colossians 1:20, 22, where that fourth term for reconciliation, *apokatallassō*, is used again. Let us read it in context:

> **1:19** For in him all the fullness of God was pleased to dwell,
>
> **1:20** and through him God was pleased to reconcile [*apokatallazai,* aorist infinitive] to himself all things, whether on earth or in heaven, by making peace through the blood of his cross.
>
> **1:21** And you who were once estranged and hostile in mind, doing evil deeds,
>
> **1:22** he has now reconciled [*apokatellazen,* aorist] in his fleshly body through death, so as to present you holy and blameless and irreproachable before him—
>
> **1:23** provided that you continue securely established and steadfast in the faith, without shifting from the hope promised by the gospel that you heard. (NRSV)

The universal and cosmic significance of God's work through Christ is in view where the passage speaks about "all things" being reconciled, "whether on earth or in heaven." Reconciliation, then, will finally involve the universe as a whole and not just believing humans; the time will come when the universe will no longer be subjected to decay or dissolution but will reflect the harmony that God originally intended for all that was created.

All in all, the actual work of reconciling requires a distinct focus and distinctive frame of reference: it requires a focus on the other person as someone of value, whatever the facts that make that person different or difficult or distant, and it requires an attitude of forgiveness and inclusiveness that can claim that person for relation and closeness. The attitude of forgiveness motivates one to set aside that which causes distance, and the spirit of inclusiveness exhibits openness by which togetherness can begin and achieve development. According to several of the texts we have examined, in Christ God has acted kindly toward us in this way, proffering forgiveness for sins, restored harmony after a life of disobedience, and peaceful relations after our selfish waywardness that displeased God. Christ acted on our behalf as God's reconciling agent.

Paul explains that having received reconciliation he had been given a ministry as a reconciler. This means that he had to learn to see other people as God sees them; he had to be open to relate to people with a view to their God-given worth, their human potential, and their deepest human need. This framework and focus is the basis for evangelism in depth and human community in full. As Howard Thurman once voiced it, "One person, standing in his [or her] own place, penetrates deeply into the life of another in a manner that makes possible an ingathering within that other life, and thus the wildness is gentled out of a personality at war with itself."[3] We too can develop this ability, this way of relating to another, provided there is, first, a deep gratitude to God for having reconciled us, and second, an intentional concern to be a reconciling person. God has been open to us. We can learn to be open to others. It begins with a simple interest to learn to be open, with a concern for people's deepest need, and it deepens through a continuing gratitude to God for accepting us as he has so graciously done. This is how, like Paul, we become "ambassadors for Christ," and work among people with "God making his appeal through us." Paul must have been seeking to underscore the importance of this when in concluding that classic passage in 2 Corinthians about reconciliation he quickly and rightly advised his readers, "We urge you also not to accept the grace of God in vain" (2 Cor. 6:1 NRSV).

II. Reconciliation: Aspects of Our Task

Our reexamination of the biblical statements and terms about reconciliation has yielded at least three results: (1) It has reminded us and clarified anew for us what reconciliation means in the vocabulary of faith; (2) it has refreshed our understanding about God's reconciling work through Christ Jesus, thus deepening our gratitude for received grace, which in turn can stir us to worship God more attentively; and (3) it has brought into sharper focus our task as reconciling agents, a task that in the press of our times calls for greater attention and more strategic action on our part.

The first and second of these results from our study are in the vertical category of our Christian experience since God and the self are related by a personal faith. The third result involves the horizontal dimension of our Christian experience since it requires interacting with other humans. The longer we consider this, the greater the awareness becomes that personal faith in Christ—the vertical dimension—and the obedient outworking of that faith in dealing with others—the horizontal dimension—*always form a cross.* This must be remembered as we go about our work in the world because reconciliation is always a costly matter. It was by cost to Jesus Christ that we were reconciled to God, and we cannot be reconciling agents in his name without undergoing some demands that will press upon us.

I deem it important in extending this line of thought to list some books that treat the theological aspects of reconciliation in greater detail than I have done here, and to list some books that can give further guidance regarding the social aspects of reconciliation than our time here allows me to treat with sufficient detail.

As for the theology of reconciliation, here are four books the reading of which can not only widen one's perspective but also deepen one's devotion:

1. Leon Morris, *The Apostolic Preaching of the Cross* (Grand Rapids: William B. Eerdmans Publishing Co., 1956).

2. Vincent Taylor, *The Cross of Christ: Eight Public Lectures* (London: Macmillan & Co., Ltd., 1957).

3. Vincent Taylor, *Forgiveness and Reconciliation: A Study in New Testament Theology* (London: Macmillan & Co., Ltd., 1960).

4. Ralph P. Martin, *Reconciliation: A Study of Paul's Theology* (London: Marshall, 1981).

These are but four books selected from among many other studies that treat the theology of reconciliation, but I believe you will find these four readily available, intellectually arresting, and theologically astute.

For insights on the social outworking of the reconciliation concern, I will list only two from among the many others available, but these are two that I rate at the top of the list:

Howard Thurman, *Disciplines of the Spirit* (New York and Evanston: Harper & Row, Publishers, 1963).

Curtiss Paul DeYoung, *Reconciliation: Our Greatest Challenge—Our Only Hope* (Valley Forge: Judson Press, 1997).

Howard Thurman (1899–1981), an African American, was a noted minister, educator, and author who in his preaching, teaching, and writings delineated, in my judgment, the most thoroughly analytical, scholarly, and practical account of how the Christian faith can inform the American democratic tradition for its fullest development. His insights were addressed to healing the deep-seated social ills of this nation, and the final chapter in his book, *Disciplines of the Spirit*, offers his counsel, derived from a fresh examination of the Christian faith allied with proofs from his own experiences, about how to become and develop as a reconciling person. Thurman delineated with clarity how and why it is that "the discipline of reconciliation for the religious [person] cannot be separated from the discipline of religious experience"[4] itself. Influenced by the account we have examined in Matthew 5:24, Thurman explained: "What a man knows as his birthright in his experience before God he must accept and affirm as his necessity in his relations with his fellows." He further explained, "This is why the way of reconciliation and the way of love finally are one way."[5] Thurman's discussion in that chapter about the discipline that *agape*-love provides in the life of someone who *wills* and *works* for reconciliation is the best I have ever read.

Curtiss Paul DeYoung, author of *Reconciliation: Our Greatest Challenge—Our Only Hope*, is Caucasian, a former student of mine, and presently serves as president of TURN Leadership Foundation, a metrowide ministry network based in Minneapolis that serves as a catalyst for reconciliation and social justice in Minneapolis and St. Paul, Minnesota. DeYoung is one of those voices of goodwill speaking out to offer guidance and give help to persons and cities experiencing social conflict. His book is his attempt to share wisdom, a wisdom that is biblical and tested in his own life struggles. This book is a logical and planned sequel to his earlier book entitled *Coming Together: The Bible's Message in an Age of Diversity*, which discussed the Bible as, in part, a record of a culturally diverse people seeking God's will, and how the person Jesus—"an Afro-Asiatic Galilean Jew," as he describes him—became a universal Christ who liberates, shapes a new and inclusive community, and empowers his followers to be agents of reconciliation. The book *Coming Together* ended with a call for reconciliation, and DeYoung's treatment in the book *Reconciliation* offers counsel on the process one must understand and follow in developing a reconciliation mind-set, entering into meaningful relationships, and taking responsibility for the polarization that exists in order to take action to shape the necessary and God-willed harmony.

There are places in his book where DeYoung calls attention to how he came to experience what he has written about, and he has written about it all with a responsible and contagious bearing. His is a holistic approach, with an accent on the discipline and cost of being a reconciler. Knowing him as I do, and knowing some of the risks he has had to take and some of what he has had to undergo as a believing, teaching, active practitioner of *agape*-love, I strongly recommend DeYoung's book on reconciliation. Based in a vital Christian faith, it offers sound guidance, a guidance that is never past tense but is contemporary, focused, creative, and practical.

I have called attention to Thurman's work and DeYoung's treatment of reconciliation because both deal necessarily, forthrightly, and helpfully with the discipline demanded for those who would work as agents of reconciliation. It is a discipline that demands realism in the face of divisive walls, hostility, and hate; a discipline that refuses to cower before the barriers that block harmony; a discipline that properly and steadily informs, encourages, and energizes one to engage in the divine process of reconciliation, that readies one to take responsibility, and, understanding the necessity for forgiveness, seeks to effect it by touching the soul, repairing the wrong that injured, and establishing the needed relationship. This discipline demands an active love, a healthy self-image, the willingness to risk oneself, and a sense of being companioned in the task by God.

A word is in order about the necessity for forgiveness in becoming reconciled, both in seeking reconciliation and in granting it. Forgiveness is that ability and active willingness to pardon someone and thus "wipe out," as it were, the reason for the discord and separation. Forgiveness demands the letting go of grudges and attitudes that block being related.

Some months ago, while reading an issue of *The Chronicle of Higher Education* (July 17, 1998), I was delightfully surprised to learn from one of its articles about some research currently underway in several universities dealing with "Forgiveness Studies."[6] In view of marital discord, families in disarray, and nations wracked by ethnic, tribal, and religious divisions, social psychologists have become increasingly concerned about the effects of anger, resentment, and the desire for revenge, among other attitudes and feelings, on mind-body connections, and how forgiveness can improve physical as well as mental health.

At the time the article appeared there were twenty-nine projects underway in universities on forgiveness research, with the John Templeton Foundation having underwritten most of the support cost. The scholars are at work conducting studies, developing inventory checklists to assess whether and how persons learn to forgive—and what they forgive; they have been busy administering tests, collecting data, organizing conferences, bringing researchers into contact with one another, and publishing preliminary reports and articles about their still embryonic science. They are concerned to define the meaning and parameters of forgiveness, the need for forgiveness, as well as the effects of forgiveness. Although most people equate this subject with religion and not science, some of the scientists have shown concern to work seriously at finding common ground between the two approaches to forgiveness. The current research is aimed at determining what forgiveness is, how it works, in which cases, and what its effects are at the level of mind-body connections.

From the standpoint of religious experience, we know that true forgiveness can and does happen in the human heart, and that emotional and behavioral changes take place in both the forgiving and the forgiven person due to the creative and healing power of love. Those persons who are deeply aware that God loves and has forgiven them seem to deal with their hurt feelings more quickly and forgive more readily. We humans can be trained to forgive, and reconciling agents must help people learn and choose to do so, but the bottom line is always that the wounded person must willingly turn away from the history of the happening, refuse to harbor resentment raised by the happening, and choose to forgive those responsible for wronging him or her. This is easier to achieve when the offending action is in the past and the offender or offenders have offered a sincere apology, but even when this has not happened, a reasonable thinking person can be predisposed in spirit to forgive. A serious believer will surely be so predisposed, instructed by the example of Jesus as he hung on his cross: "Father, forgive them; for they do not know what they are doing" (Luke 23:34*a* NRSV).

As church leaders, we will all readily agree that the church has a potential—and mandated—role in bringing people together, to help people experience forgiveness, both the forgiveness God grants and the forgiveness needed from other people. And we must remain mindful of our Lord's encouraging pronouncement: "Blessed are the peacemakers, for they will be called children of God" (Matt. 5:9 NRSV). This beatitude is preserved only in Matthew's account of the Sermon on the Mount and seems addressed to those who have a heart for helping others to become reconciled. In the setting of that day, it could as well have been a word of caution to those in the listening crowd who were of a zealotic bent, those listeners who were sympathetic to militaristic attempts to remove the yoke of Roman rule from the Jewish nation's neck. Was this a warning word from Jesus that the only holy crusades are crusades for peace? The political environment of our Lord's ministry should never be overlooked in studying what he taught and how he taught.[7] In this beatitude Jesus tells us all that God's kingdom is not promoted by human violence, that peacemaking is the way to shape the best future, and those who do this work of effecting reconciliation are God's true children.

In light of this, it is important to reflect on how often this emphasis on being peaceful or on making peace appears in the New Testament. Consider Mark 9:50*b:* "Be at peace with one another" (NRSV). Interestingly, this exhortation is linked in that verse with Jesus's instruction that we are to be like salt in the world. Here is the full saying:

Mark 9:50 Salt is good, but if salt has lost its saltiness, how can you season it? Have salt in yourselves, and be at peace with one another (NRSV).

There are two passages in Romans with this emphasis:

Romans 12:18 If it is possible, so far as it depends on you, live peaceably with all (NRSV).

Romans 14:19 Let us then pursue what makes for peace and for mutual upbuilding (NRSV).

In **2 Corinthians 13:11** we are told: "Agree with one another, live in peace; and the God of love and peace will be with you" (NRSV) and **1 Thessalonians 5:13***b* exhorts us: "Be at peace among yourselves" (NRSV). **Hebrews 12:14** offers the same directive, with a reminder about right living: "Pursue peace with everyone, and the holiness without which no one will see the Lord" (NRSV). Then there is that illuminating statement in James 3:18, part of a set of pointed instructions to a group of believers fractured by religious, economic, and social differences: "And a harvest of righteousness [or: the fruit of justice] is sown in peace for those who make peace" (NRSV). The message in the image is that righteousness makes its presence known and felt through peace. This line in James 3:18 is like the teaching of Jesus in the seventh beatitude, and it simply reports that peacemaking is the highest activity and the greatest deed, that the truly righteous person promotes peace.

All of us will readily recall the well-publicized news we received in June of 1995 after the Southern Baptist Convention, the largest Protestant denomination in the United States, at their annual meeting passed a resolution of repentance for their denomination's involvement in and support of slavery, one of the contributing causes for founding the Convention one hundred and fifty years earlier. A public apology was made to African Americans, whose ancestors suffered under that pernicious system. The Convention sought forgiveness for justifying the slavery system, for involvement in the segregating system that followed slavery, and for their part in the history that shaped the racist climate that still afflicts this nation. The concern was reconciliation, and forgiveness was being sought in order to experience this benefit and need.

There were critics who viewed the Convention resolution with suspicion, coming so late as it did in the group's history, but I viewed the apology as responsible and honest. It is never too late to right a wrong, however long-standing, and the delegates were attempting to do so. That resolution of apology would never have happened apart from an announced "change of heart." Over time, the Southern Baptist Convention was readied for reconciliation, and it took more than one influencing factor: it took the impact of a more enlightened public, it took the legal overthrow of segregation, and it took a heightened moral and social conscience, among other things, but I must also highlight the critical influence upon the Convention's members of a more informed and humane reading of the Scriptures and the steady ministry of the Spirit of God who works always to effect reconciliation.

Our Lord's mandate that we evangelize (Matt. 28:18–20) is at one with our assignment to be reconcilers (2 Cor. 5:19–20). Both service roles have been entrusted to us, and both are strategically related in two ways: first, the same message that brings salvation is the basis for reconciliation not only with God but with other persons; and second, the same *agape*-love that motivates us to evangelize also motivates us to be reconciling agents. These two ministries might well be described as two sides of one coin since they are so closely conjoined for believers.

The ministry of evangelizing and the ministry of reconciling both call for a knowledgeable, earnest, patient, persistent, and unselfish spirit of caring about people. The caring must be strong and steady because evil forces do not yield their control without a fight, and destructive hostilities and entrenched angers are never scared off by just a Christian presence, however right our cause. We must be armed with meanings that matter, use apt methods to share those meanings, and we must care deeply enough for people in order to deal effectively with the attitudes, feelings, and other fall-out from the deep consciousness people have of personal offenses suffered and the threats people fear because of color differences and cultural diversities. I say this because these problems continue to be more determinative when people meet each other than the more reasonable goal of finding a common ground for relating peacefully and fruitfully. Remembered injuries and differences in color and culture continue to predispose people to negate, exclude, or fight rather than seek peace. Our mandate to evangelize and our mission to reconcile authorize and empower us to break through the walls that block people from the harmony we so sorely need in this world.

We have noted earlier that reconciliation cannot be achieved without an active willingness to seek forgiveness and to forgive. As reconcilers, we can help persons reach and act out that willingness. In addition, and in the interest of maintaining harmony, we must help persons recognize, admit, and overcome their prejudices and learn to discipline their preferences. I will spare you further talk about prejudices, about which we hear more often, but something must be said here about preferences, since these can also block right relations between people.

The dictionary defines a *preference* as "a greater liking; a first choice; a giving of priority or advantage to someone or something." We all know what it means to put one thing ahead of something else, as when choosing a car, a certain kind and size of house, a college or university to attend, to name a few instances. We exercised a preference when dating, which led to courtship and marriage. Preferences are very personal matters; they are daily concerns in the business of living and relating. We know what it is to enjoy having and doing what we prefer, and we know what it is to endure not having our likes and chosen priorities fulfilled. Preferences are part of our personality-system, and their roots extend deep into the soil that nurtured our personal growth.

Preferences must be understood and valued for what they are and for what they enable us to be and do. But preferences must also be scrutinized because they bias us; they slant us within, so that our interests, concerns, attitudes, and judgments about things will lean in a certain direction. Preferences must be measured and tested by something higher than our "likes" and "dislikes" and personal priorities lest we find ourselves living really by prejudices. Unexamined preferences can be socially problematic. They can influence us, unwittingly, to act unwisely in some matter, or to give priority to some concern that does not promote peace but discord. A preference must be honored when it is just and unselfish, but it should be changed when it makes one selfishly judgmental, racist, and socially prohibitive. So much goes into the molding of our lives, and that molding produces consequences in us that we follow mostly without thinking—until we are stirred by something that forces us to think about those consequences.[8]

Growing up, as we did, in some national, ethnic, racial, cultural, geographical, and denominational setting, we all tend to honor and prefer that setting and we tend to judge all else and all others by what that setting means to us. The time comes, however, when we are stirred by something to think more deeply about what conditioned us, and we find it necessary to alter our view about some matter or resist some influence that conditioned us improperly for responding openly, peacefully, and helpfully in the places where we now find ourselves. The conditioning is there inside us, and it stays there, steadily influencing us, until we see it for what it is and deal with it and ourselves, affirming what we should and altering what we must. Reconciliation is achieved only when we are no longer limited to or bound by what conditioned us against relating to others. And the fruits of reconciliation can only grow when we are disciplined and kept under management by a strong ethic for staying in relation.

I have quoted much from the writings of Paul during our time together, and with understood reasons. As we prepare to conclude this time of study, let us be reminded of Paul's declaration about how he handled his prior conditioning as a Hebrew as he dealt with the wider world of differing groups in the Roman Empire; it is a declaration about the principle that disciplined his preferences and kept him open as a relational and reconciling person: That declaration is found in 1 Corinthians 9:19–23:

1 Cor. 9:19 For though I am free with respect to all, I have made myself a slave to all, so that I might win more of them.

9:20 To the Jews I became as a Jew, in order to win Jews. To those under the law I became as one under the law (though I myself am not under the law) so that I might win those under the law.

9:21 To those outside the law I became as one outside the law (though I am not free from God's law but am under Christ's law) so that I might win those outside the law.

9:22 To the weak I became weak, that I might win the weak. I have become all things to all people, that I might by all means save some.

9:23 I do it all for the sake of the gospel, so that I may share in its blessings. (NRSV)

Such was Paul's approach to handling his preferences; he kept those preferences ordered and informed by the higher principle of the relational imperative of *agape*-love. This kind of caring-sharing love does not concern itself with social expediency but with spiritual necessity and the best human future. So it was truly the case with Paul, as he confessed to his Corinthian readers in that classic passage we examined earlier: "From now on, therefore, we regard no one from a human point of view; even though we once knew Christ from a human point of view, we know him no longer in that way. So if anyone is in Christ, there is a new creation: everything old has passed away; see, everything has become new! All this is from God, who reconciled us to himself through Christ, and has given us the ministry of reconciliation; that is, in Christ God was reconciling the world to himself, not counting their trespasses against them, and entrusting the message of reconciliation to us. So we are ambassadors for Christ, since God is making his appeal through us; . . ." (2 Cor. 5:16–20a NRSV). May this be the case with us as well.

Appendix

Resolution on Racial Reconciliation on the 150th Anniversary of the Southern Baptist Convention

WHEREAS, since its founding in 1845, the Southern Baptist Convention has been an effective instrument of God in missions, evangelism, and social ministry; and

WHEREAS, the Scriptures teach that Eve is the mother of all living (Gen. 3:20), and that God shows no partiality, but in every nation whoever fears him and works righteousness is accepted by him (Acts 10:34–35), and that God has made from one blood every nation of men to dwell on the face of the earth (Acts 17:26); and

WHEREAS, our relationship to African-Americans has been hindered from the beginning by the role that slavery played in the formation of the Southern Baptist Convention and

WHEREAS, many of our Southern Baptist forebears defended the right to own slaves, and either participated in, supported, or acquiesced in the particularly inhumane nature of American slavery; and

WHEREAS, in later years Southern Baptists failed, in many cases, to support, and in some cases opposed, legitimate initiatives to secure the civil rights of African-Americans; and

WHEREAS, racism has led to discrimination, oppression, injustice, and violence, both the Civil War and throughout the history of our nation; and

WHEREAS, racism has divided the body of Christ and Southern Baptists in particular, and separated us from our African-American brothers and sisters; and

WHEREAS, many of our congregations have intentionally and/or unintentionally excluded African-Americans from worship, membership, and leadership; and

WHEREAS, racism profoundly distorts our understanding of Christian morality, leading some Southern Baptists to believe that racial prejudice and discrimination are compatible with the Gospel; and

WHEREAS, Jesus performed the ministry of reconciliation to restore sinners to a right relationship with the heavenly Father, and to establish right relations among all human beings, especially within the family of faith.

Therefore, be it RESOLVED, that we, the messengers to the Sesquicentennial meeting of the Southern Baptist Convention, assembled in Atlanta, Georgia, June 20–22, 1995, unwaveringly denounce racism, in all its forms, as deplorable sin; and

Be if further RESOLVED, that we affirm the Bible's teaching that every human life is sacred, and is of equal and immeasurable worth, made in God's image, regardless of race or ethnicity (Gen. 1:27), and that, with respect to salvation through Christ, there is neither Jew nor Greek, there is neither slave nor free, there is neither male nor female, for (we) are all one in Christ Jesus (Gal. 3:28); and

Be if further RESOLVED, that we lament and repudiate historic acts of evil such as slavery from which we continue to reap a bitter harvest, and we recognize that the racism which yet plagues our culture today is inextricably tied to the past; and

Be it further RESOLVED, that we apologize to all African-Americans for condoning and/or perpetuating individual and systemic racism in our lifetime; and we genuinely repent of racism of which we have been guilty, whether consciously (Ps. 19:13) or unconsciously (Lev. 4:27); and

Be it further RESOLVED, that we ask forgiveness from our African-American brothers and sisters, acknowledging that our own healing is at stake; and

Be it further RESOLVED, that we hereby commit ourselves to eradicate racism in all its forms from the Southern Baptist life and ministry; and

Be it further RESOLVED, that we commit ourselves to be doers of the Word (James 1:22) by pursuing racial reconciliation in all our relationships, especially with our brothers and sisters in Christ (1 John 2:6), to the end that our light would so shine before others, that they may see (our) good works and glorify (our) Father in heaven (Matt. 5:16); and

Be it finally RESOLVED, that we pledge our commitment to the Great Commission task of making disciples of all peoples (Matt. 28:19), confessing that in the church God is calling together one people from every tribe and nation (Rev. 5:9), and proclaiming that the Gospel of our Lord Jesus Christ is the only certain and sufficient ground upon which redeemed persons will stand together in restored family union as joint-heirs with Christ (Rom. 8:17).

   —Adopted by the Southern Baptist Convention
     June 20–22, 1995, Atlanta, Georgia

Notes

Chapter 2

1. T. S. Eliot, "The Idea of a Christian Society," in *Christianity and Culture* (New York: Harcourt, Brace and World, 1949).

2. Ronald Berman, ed., *Solzhenitsyn at Harvard* (Washington, D.C.: Ethics and Public Policy Center, 1980), 16–17.

3. Quoted in Taylor Branch, *Parting the Waters: America in the King Years 1954–63* (New York: Simon and Schuster, 1988), 700–701.

4. Richard John Neuhaus, *The Naked Public Square: Religion and Democracy in America* (Grand Rapids: Wm. B. Eerdmans, 1984), 97–98.

5. Ibid., 98.

6. Quoted in *Dallas Morning News,* Nov. 20, 1988, p. 2A.

7. Dr. King spoke for an hour and received a standing ovation at the conclusion of his message. Dr. King was leaving the seminary campus and going directly to meet with Louisville's mayor and civic leaders. Knowing this, the seminary students presented Dr. King with a previously prepared petition signed by approximately 250 students, calling on the mayor to integrate all municipal facilities in Louisville.

8. Lillian Smith, *Killers of the Dream* (Garden City, N.Y.:

Anchor Books, 1963 ed.), 17, 27–28, 81. Originally published in 1949.

9. Ibid., 28.

10. "Martin Luther King, Jr." *World Book Encyclopedia,* Vol. XI. For a full text of this speech, see a reprint in the Christian Life Commission's LIGHT (January 1984). Cf. Taylor Branch, *Parting the Waters,* pp. 846 and following for the fascinating background leading up to this speech.

Chapter 4

1. Frank E. Gaebelein, gen. ed., *The Expositor's Bible Commentary,* vol. 9 (Grand Rapids: Regency Reference Library, 1981), 476.

2. © 1966 by F.E.L. Publication. All Rights Reserved.

Chapter 5

1. Howard Thurman, *Jesus and the Disinherited* (Boston: Beacon Press, 1996), pp. 104–5.

2. Paul Hoon, "First John: Exposition," in *The Interpreter's Bible* (Nashville: Abingdon, 1957), 12:260–61.

Chapter 16

1. *The Birmingham News,* January 17, 1999, p. A17.

2. *The Birmingham Post-Herald,* July 9, 1996, p. A3.

3. *The Birmingham News,* July 30, 1996, p. 52.

4. *The Reader's Digest Great Encyclopedic Dictionary,* p. 1109.

5. *The New York Times,* January 27, 1999, p. A28.

6. "Resolution on Racial Reconciliation," Southern Baptist Convention, Atlanta, Georgia, June 22, 1995. See complete text at end of this book.

7. *The Baptist Standard,* January 20, 1999, p. 1.

8. Ibid., p. 3.

9. Ibid.

Reconciliation: Two Biblical Studies

1. James Barr, *The Semantics of Biblical Language* (Oxford University Press, 1961), p. vii.

2. Vincent Taylor, *The Cross of Christ* (London: Macmillan and Co., Ltd., 1957), p. 87. For some additional treatments of reconciliation as related to the church's teaching on atonement, see also Vincent Taylor, *Forgiveness and Reconciliation: A Study in New Testament Theology* (London: Macmillan and Co., Ltd., 1960), esp. pp. 70–108; Leon Morris, *The Apostolic Preaching of the Cross* (Grand Rapids: William B. Eerdmans Publishing Co., 1956); Ralph P. Martin, *Reconciliation: A Study of Paul's Theology* (London: Marshall, 1981).

3. Howard Thurman, *Disciplines of the Spirit* (New York: Harper & Row, Publishers, 1963), p. 108.

4. Ibid., p. 121.

5. Ibid., p. 122.

6. Scott Heller, "Emerging Field of Forgiveness Studies Explores How We Let Go of Grudges," *The Chronicle of Higher Education,* July 17, 1998, see pp. A18–A20.

7. On this, see especially Howard Thurman, *Jesus and the Disinherited* (Nashville: Abingdon Press, 1949); Alan Richardson, *The Political Christ* (Philadelphia: The Westminster Press, 1973).

8. For more on this, see H. Richard Neibuhr, *The Responsible Self* (New York: Harper & Row, Publishers, 1963), esp. pp. 42–68.

261.8348
G 349

LINCOLN CHRISTIAN COLLEGE AND SEMINARY

117903

3 4711 00180 2984